ALEXANDER
PUSHKIN

RUSSIAN CLASSICS

RADUGA PUBLISHERS MOSCOW 2001

RUSSIAN CLASSICS

ALEXANDER
PUSHKIN

SELECTED WORKS
POETRY

RADUGA PUBLISHERS MOSCOW 2001

ББК 84. Р 1-5
   П 91

Translated from the Russian
Designed by *E. Kouznetzova*

Александр Пушкин

ИЗБРАННЫЕ ПРОИЗВЕДЕНИЯ. ПОЭЗИЯ

На английском языке

First printing 1974

On the cover:
Pushkin's portrait by V. Tropinin (*a fragment*)
and the illustration to «The Bronze Horseman» by A. Benois

ISBN 5-05-004812-5

CONTENTS

Lyric Poems

Narrative Poems

Dramas

Tales in Verse

LYRIC POEMS

To Chaadayev

Not long did youth's vain hopes delude us,
Its dreams of love and prideful fame.
They briefly, fleetingly pursued us,
Then passed like mist and no more came.
But still we chafe, our hearts afire,
Under the yoke of tyranny,
And, heedful of our country's plea,
Her true deliverance desire.
We freedom wait with all the fever,
The hidden ache and eagerness
That 'fore the hour of promised bliss
Consume the young and ardent lover.
While freedom's flame within us lives,
While we by honour's voice are guided,
To Russia, comrade, let us give
Our spirits whole and undivided.
Dear friend, have faith: the wakeful skies
Presage a dawn of wonder—Russia
Shall from her age-old sleep arise,
And despotism impatient crushing,
Upon its ruins our names incise!

1818

* * *

    Light wanes, in sudden haste retreating,
And darkness clothes in haze the blue of sky and sea.
Blow, winds! Fill, sails, their charge obedient meeting,
Roll, gloomy waves, and play in furtive, fitful glee!
        A southern land, a land enchanted,
My heart with longing filled, I see before me lie;
I gaze on it, enthralled, by wayward memory
        To shores left far behind transplanted...
Anew am I aflame; from out my eyes well tears;
        My heart now sinks, now soars in rapture;
Past dreams and fancies hover round me; I recapture
The mad, tempestuous love of half-forgotten years
With all its sufferings, its joys, however fleeting,
Its forfeited desires and hopes illusory...
Blow, winds! Fill, sails, their charge obedient meeting,
Roll, gloomy waves, and play in furtive, fitful glee!
Fly, ship, and carry me to shores in distance shrouded
Wherever frowning seas capriciously command,
        But shun, I beg, the sorrow-clouded,
        Dim reaches of my native land,
        Where my heart's smouldering flames were fanned
        To passion, where the muses tender
Upon me smiled, where early did its bloom surrender,
        By storms incessant buffeted,
        My wasted youth, where joy light-winged
Betrayed my eager heart and brought distress that lingered
And, cruel, would not pass... 'Twas then from you I fled,

O, homeland mine, in desperation;
And you, of transient youth the transient friends,
Wooers of delight, in quest of new sensation
Far from your side I went... Wherever fortune sends,
There willing now I fly, rejecting the temptation
Held lightly out by those with whom I shared 'thout love
Sin's most delicious pleasures and who robbed me of
Fame, freedom, calm and peace; with you my bonds
                                                  I sever,
O faithless playmates mine, and leave behind for ever
Our frolics... But of pain my heart is still not free;
Its wounds remain unhealed, my fondest hopes
                                        defeating...
Blow, winds! Fill, sails, their charge obedient meeting,
Roll, gloomy waves, and play in furtive, fitful glee!..

1820

* * *

The flying wrack of clouds grows flimsier far.
O limpid star of sorrows, evening star!
Your rays have touched the autumn plains to silver,
The black heights of the rocks, the dreaming river.
Your feeble gleam in the night sky I love.
It prompts long-sleeping thoughts to stir and move,
As I recall, familiar Orb, your rising
Above that peaceful land, all joys comprising,
Where slender poplar in the valley grows,
Where tender myrtle and dark cypress doze,
And languorously the Southern seas are breaking.
There once strolled I, languidly cogitating,
High in the mountains, far above the sea.
Till, as the dusk flowed over vale and lea,
A maiden through the murk to seek you came
And told her fair friends how you bear her name.

1820

The Captive

A captive, alone in a dungeon I dwell,
Entombed in the stillness and murk of a cell.
Outside, in the courtyard, in wild, frenzied play,
My comrade, an eagle, has punced on his prey.

Then, leaving it, at me he looks as if he
In thought and in purpose at one were with me.
He looks at me so, and he utters a cry.
"'Tis time," he is saying, "from here let us fly!

"We're both wed to freedom, so let us away
To where lonely storm clouds courageously stray,
Where turbulent seas rush to merge with the sky,
Where only the winds dare to venture and I!.."

1822

Night

My voice, to which love lends a tenderness and yearning,
Disturbs night's dreamy calm... Pale at my bedside burning,
A taper wastes away... From out my heart there surge
Swift verses, streams of love, that hum and sing and merge
And, full of you, rush on, with passion overflowing.
I seem to see your eyes that, in the darkness glowing,
Meet mine... I see your smile... You speak to me alone:
My friend, my dearest friend ... I love ... I'm yours ...
                                                                    your own.

1823

Farewell to the Sea

Farewell, ye proudly rolling waters,
Farewell, thou glittering, charging sea,
The blue expanse that knows no fetters,
The beauty full of majesty.

No more will I thy friendly murmur,
Thy loud yet wistful summons hear,
Thy voice's lilt, its mournful tremor
That now, in parting, haunts my ear.

O realm that held my heart contented!
How oft, by secret dreams enthralled
And vague and misty thoughts tormented,
Thy shores I walked for hours untold.

I loved thy raucous voice, the mellow
Play of thy waves, their darts and leaps,
Thy evening calm, thy fitful sleep,
Thy passionate and wrathful bellow!

A humble fishing boat doth glide
O'er thy waves easily, obeying
Their whim, but, with the wind allied,
Great ships engulfest thou, displaying
Ungoverned rage and savage pride!

How futile proved my hope this languid
And torpid shore to leave fore'er,
To drink thy beauty in and sing it
And fly away over thy winged,
Thy soaring peaks and reaches bare!

I strove, thy eager summons hearing,
To burst my chains, but strove in vain.
By passion held, my heart ensnaring,
Here on these shores did I remain.

Ah, well, what use regret and whither
Shall I pursue my carefree way?..
One speck upon these wastes of water
Still holds my anxious heart in sway—

One cliff, one isle, a tomb of glory,
Where ebbed of lofty memories
The tide, and where Napoleon's weary
And tortured heart at last found peace.

He died, and like a tempest sweeping
From sight, so did another bold
And mighty genius leave us, keeping
On our hearts an eternal hold.

His laurel wreath behind him leaving,
He vanished, mourned by freedom... Weep
For him who was thy bard, relieving
Thy pain in storm, o mighty deep!

By thee his spirit was enchanted,
By thee 'twas sought, by thee 'twas claimed.
Like thine, 'twas fierce, like thine, undaunted,
Like thine, rebellious and untamed.

The world's a void... Where wouldst thou labour
O sea, to carry me?.. Behold!
Man's fate is uniform all over:
Where good sprouts forth, child of endeavour,
There either despots rule or gold.

Farewell, farewell! Forget I'll never
Thy solemn beauty, prideful sea!
Where'er I go, my heart aquiver,
I'll hear thee softly speak to me.

Away with me into the silence
Of flowering fields and shady groves
I'll take thy voice's magic cadence,
Thy shimmering waves and rocky coves.

1824

To the Fountain of Bakhchisarai

Two roses do I bring to thee,
O fount of love that 'fore me dances.
Thy tears poetic comfort me,
Thy tender voice my soul entrances.

Thou greetest me as I draw near,
My face with silvered dew drops spraying.
Flow, flow, O fount, and, ceaseless playing,
Speak, speak thy story in my ear.

O fount of love, O fount of sadness,
From thy stone lips long tales I heard
Of far-off parts, of woe and gladness,
But of Maria ne'er a word...

Like poor and long forgot Zarema,
Is she, the harem's pallid sun,
Formed of the mists of idle dreaming
And of the stuff of visions spun?

The spirit's dim and vague ideal
Drawn by the hand of fantasy,
Is she a thing remote, unreal,
A phantom that must cease to be?..

1824

To***

O wondrous moment! There before me,
A radiant, fleeting dream, you stood,
A vision fancy fashioned for me,
A glimpse of perfect womanhood.

Through all life's sadness, all its wonted
And hopeless flurry and unrest
Your lovely face my spirit haunted,
Your tender voice my ear caressed.

Swift storms struck; o'er me wrathful breaking,
They fast dispelled the dreams of yore.
Your image blurred, my heart forsaking,
Your voice caressed my ear no more.

In cold and gloomy isolation
The years sped by, the lonely years,
Thout deity, 'thout inspiration,
Bereft of life and love and tears.

And then—O bliss!—time's flight defeating,
You came again and 'fore me stood,
A vision radiant and fleeting,
A glimpse of perfect womanhood.

My heart is filled with sweet elation,
Anew it craves, anew reveres,
And is awake to inspiration,
Awake to life and love and tears.

1825

Winter Evening

O'er the earth a storm is prowling,
Bringing whirling, blinding snow.
Like a beast I hear it howling,
Like an infant wailing low.
Now the thatch it rustles, playing
On our roof; now at our pane
Raps like someone homeward straying
And benighted in the plain.

Old our hut is, dark and dreary,
By a candle dimly lit...
Why so sad, my dear, and weary
At the window do you sit?
Is't because the storm is moaning
That so very still you keep?
Does your spindle's mournful droning
Put you quietly to sleep?

Come, O comrade solitary
Of this cheerless youth of mine,
Take a cup, and let us bury
All our many woes in wine!
Of a maid out by a river
Sing a little song to me
Or a tomtit, one that never
Leaves its home beyond the sea.

O'er the earth a storm is prowling,
Bringing whirling, blinding snow.
Like a beast I hear it howling,
Like an infant wailing low.
Come, O comrade solitary
Of this cheerless youth of mine,
Take a cup and let us bury
All our many woes in wine!

1825

Bacchanal Song

Why, revelry's voice, are you still?
Ring out, songs of Bacchus, our patron!
Long life to you, maiden and matron,
Ye fair ones who gave of your love with a will!
  Drink, friend, drink with gusto and relish!
    As I do in mine,
    In your glass of wine
  Fling lightly the ring that you cherish!
Come, let's clink our glasses and high let us raise them!
Hail, muses! Hail, reason! In song let us praise them!
  Thou, bright sun of genius, shine on!
  Like this ancient lamp that grows dimmer
  And fades with the coming of dawn,
So false wisdom pales at the first flash and glimmer
  Of true wisdom's ne'er-fading light...
Live, radiant day! Perish, darkness and night!

1825

The Prophet

My lonely heart athirst, I trod
A barren waste when, so 'twas fated,
A wingéd seraph 'fore me stood:
Where crossed the desert roads he waited.
Upon my orbs of sightless clay
His fingers lightly he did lay.
And like a startled eagle round me
I gazed and saw the earth surrounded,
Hemmed in by sky... He touched my ear,
Then t'other, and, most marked and clear,
There came to me the gentle flutter
Of angels' wings, I heard the vine
Push through the earth and skyward climb,
The deep-sea monsters in the water
Like tiny fishes glide... And o'er
Me calm he bent and out he tore
My sinful tongue... Not once withdrawing
His gaze from mine, he pushed, unseen,
A serpent's deadly sting between
My ice-cold lips... Then, swiftly drawing
His shining sword, he clove my breast,
Plucked out my quivering heart, and, sombre
And grim of aspect, coolly thrust
Into the gaping hole an ember
That ran with flame... I lay there, dead,
And God, God spake, and this He said:
"Arise, O sage! My summons hearing,
Do as I bid, by naught deterred;
Stride o'er the earth, a prophet, searing
The hearts of men with righteous word."

1826

Wintry Road

Slow the moon, embraced by shadow,
Climbs the hilly clouds of night
And upon the cheerless meadow
Sadly pours its pallid light.

Down the road, as white and eerie
As the wintry, boundless lea,
Runs my troika, and the weary
Sleigh-bell jangles drowsily.

In the driver's song unending
Much is there that speaks to me,
Now a plaint, my spirit rending,
Now a reckless gaiety...

All around is snow, and nothing,
Not a light to cheer the eye;
Mileposts rush to meet me, nodding
As they pass indifferent by.

But, my Nina, on the morrow,
By the fire's unsteady blaze,
I will drown my gloom, my sorrow
And my dullness in your gaze.

Let the clock, its passage charted,
Midnight strike; we'll not, my own,
Once the others leave, be parted,
But stay on—stay on alone.

Sad am I... The night encloses
Field and wood... The moon looms wan...
In his seat the driver dozes,
Through the snow the road drags on.

1826

To My Nanny

Dear doting sweetheart of my childhood,
Companion of my austere fate!
In the lone house deep in the wild wood
How patiently for me you wait.
Alone beside your window sitting
You wait for me and blame the clock,
While, in your wrinkled hands, your knitting
Fitfully falters to a stop.
Beyond the crumbling gates the pinetrees
Shadow the road you watch so well.
Nameless forebodings, dark anxieties,
Oppress your heart. You cannot tell
What visions haunt you: Now you seem to
see...

1826

* * *

Deep in Siberia's mines, let naught
Subdue your proud and patient spirit.
Your crushing toil and lofty thought
Shall not be wasted—do not fear it.

Misfortune's sister, hope sublime,
From sombre dungeon pain will banish;
Joy will awake and sorrow vanish...
 Twill come, the promised, longed-for time;

The heavy locks will burst—rejoice!—
And love and friendship 'thout delusion
Will reach you in your grim seclusion
As does my freedom-loving voice.

The prison walls will crash... Content,
At door will freedom wait to meet you;
Your brothers, hastening to greet you,
To you the sword will glad present.

1827

Arion

We many were who filled the boat:
Some held the sails aloft and flying,
Some plied the oars, and thus, defying,
The wayward winds, kept us afloat.
Our helmsman steered the vessel, loaded
Full as she was, and onward sent;
And I, to them I sang, content
And unconcerned... A violent
Gale overtook the boat and goaded
The seas to fury... All were lost
But I who out the deep was tossed
By surging waves; my body flinging
On to the sands, they fled... Now I
Sit drying in the sun and my
Old, well loved songs in relish singing.

1827

* * *

Sing, lovely one, I beg, no more
The songs of Georgia in my presence,
For of a distant life and shore
Their mournful sound calls up remembrance;

For of a moonlit steppe, and night
They cruelly, vengefully remind me,
And of a face long lost to sight,
Well loved, but left, alas, behind me.

When you are nigh, I gaze at you,
And lo! No fatal shadow haunts me.
But at your song's first note, anew
It reappears, and plagues and taunts me.

Sing, lovely one, I beg, no more
The songs of Georgia in my presence,
For of a distant life and shore
Their mournful sound calls up remembrance.

1828

Antiar

On sands where sunshine is a curse,
Antiar, a sentry grim and dreaded,
Alone in all the universe,
Stands, to the arid stillness wedded.

The thirsting steppes gave birth to him,
The sun above them gleaming redly,
And, spiteful, fed his roots and limbs
With poisons swift to act and deadly.

The venom, seeping through his bark,
Melts in the blaze and heat of morning,
But thickens at the fall of dark,
With crystal drops the tree adorning.

No birds, no beasts dare venture near.
Black winds alone, not lightly daunted,
Rush up, but fly away in fear,
By his malignant vapours tainted.

And when a rain-cloud sprays his crown
And leaves the heavy branches sodden,
The drops that from the tree stream down
With poisons are already laden.

But man bade man to seek Antiar—
One look sufficed... The slave, past caring,

Set out, and though the way was far,
Returned at dawn, the poison bearing.

A branch and resin 'fore his lord
He placed in silent supplication,
And down his ashen brow there poured
Cold, leaden drops of perspiration.

And, falling weakly on a mat,
His face a mask of sickly pallor,
He died, a humble bondsman, at
The feet of an almighty ruler.

With poison did his henchmen smear
The prince's arrows at his orders,
And to his neighbours far and near
Death sent he forth across the borders.

1828

*   *   *

Upon the hills of Georgia lies the haze of night...
    Below, *Aragva* foams... The sadness
That fills the void of days is, strangely, half delight,
    'Tis both sweet pain and sweeter gladness.
Because you haunt my heart, it cannot be at rest,
    And yet 'tis light, and untormented
By morbid thoughts... It loves... It loves because it must,
    Rejoicing in the love by fortune sent it.

1829

Winter Morning

Snow, frost and sunshine: lovely morning!
Yet you, dear love, its magic scorning,
Are still abed... Awake, my sweet!..
Cast sleep away, I beg, and, rising,
Yourself a northern star, the blazing
Aurora, northern beauty, meet.

Last night, a snow-storm raged, remember;
A turbid haze swam in the sombre,
Wind-ravaged sky, and through the grey
Murk of the clouds the moon shone dully,
And you sat listless, melancholy...
But now—look out the window, pray—

'Neath lucid skies of clearest azure,
Great snowy carpets, winter's treasure,
A rich and dazzling sight, lie spread.
The wood is etched against them darkly,
The firs, rime-starred, are green and sparkling,
In shiny mail the stream is clad.

A mellow glow like that of amber
Illumes the room... 'Tis good to linger
Beside the gaily crackling stove,
And think and dream... But let our honest
Brown mare without delay be harnessed
That we may take a sledge ride, love.

We'll give free rein to her, and lightly,
The snow of morning gleaming brightly,
Skim over it, and, full of glee,
Cross empty fields and empty meadows,
A once green wood with trees like shadows,
A stream and bank long dear to me.

1829

* * *

I loved you, and that love, to die refusing,
May still—who knows!—be smouldering
                              in my breast
Pray be not pained—believe me, of my choosing
I'd never have you troubled or distressed.
I loved you mutely, hopelessly and truly,
With shy yet fervent tenderness aglow;
Mine was a jealous passion and unruly...
May God grant that another will love you so!

1829

* * *

Whether the streets I roam, a crowded
Church enter, or drown care with friends,
It matters not: e'er am I hounded
By thought of life and of its end.

This do I think: swift is life's passage,
And all of us now gathered here
Will glimpse ere long Death's dreaded visage;
Already someone's hour draws near.

Upon an ancient oak-tree gazing,
I whisper, awed: "When I am gone
It will be here, the woodland gracing;
My fathers went—the tree grows on!"

And playing with a child, I murmur:
"Farewell!.. My place I cede... The hour
Is close at hand—My life is over—
For me to rot, for you to flower."

Each day, each year that passes, transient,
I follow mute to its decline,
The moment of my doom, impatient,
In vain attempting to divine.

Will I be claimed by death in warfare,
Whilst on my travels? Mid the waves?

Or will a neighbouring valley offer
My cold remains a quiet grave?

Where to be laid in sleep eternal
Is all the same to lifeless clay.
Yet 'tis beneath the skies maternal
That I would rest...
                    Day upon day

Over my tomb let Life, e'er youthful,
A fountain, flow in sheer delight,
And Nature, beautiful and wistful,
Shed upon all its dazzling light.

1829

The Caucasus

Below me the silver-capped Caucasus lies...
Nearby an abyss yawns, and, far down, a roaring
Stream swift rushes past; o'er the peaks calmly soaring,
An eagle seems motionless, pinned to the skies.
Here rivers are born that mid rocks, grumbling, wander
And landslides begin with a crash of thunder.

Here float solemn storm-clouds, and through them cascade
Swift torrents of water; they plunge o'er the edges
Of great, naked cliffs and spill down to the ledges
That patches of moss and dry brushwood invade.
Beneath spread green groves, lush with herbs and
                                                     sweet-scented,
Where birds trill and chirp and where deer play, contented.

Lower still, in the hills, nestle men; flocks of sheep
The pasturelands roam; to the gay, flowery meadow
Where flows the Aragva, its banks clothed in shadow,
A shepherd descends. In a narrow and deep
Ravine a poor horseman lurks, tense and unsleeping,
And, laugh-crazed, the Terek goes tumbling and leaping.

It lashes about like a beast in a cage
With food out of reach, full of hunger and craving,
And licks at the boulders, and howling and raving,
Strikes out at the shore in a frenzy and rage.
Alas! it is thwarted: the mountains surround it;
Mute, threatening giants, they press darkly round it.

1829

*   *   *

When in my arms your slender form
I take, perhaps a shade too boldly,
And words of love, impetuous, warm,
Pour out to you, in silence, coldly
From my unasked-for, rash embrace
You free yourself, and for an instant
A smile appears upon your face,
At once mistrustful, wan and distant.
Too promptly has your memory stored
Of all my errant ways the rumour—
I speak, and you are out of humour,
I plead my cause, and you are bored...
O how I curse the sweet diversions
And pleasures of my wicked youth,
Love's nightly meetings and excursions
To some dark garden nook or path,
The verses born to stimulate
And stir the blood, the fond caresses
Bestowed too soon by trusting lasses,
And their laments that came too late.

1830

* * *

What means my name to you?.. 'Twil die
As does the melancholy rumour
Of distant waves or, of a summer,
The forest's hushed nocturnal sigh.

Found on a fading album page,
Dim will it seem and enigmatic,
Like words traced on a tomb, a relic
Of some long dead and vanished age.

What's in my name?.. Long since forgot,
Erased by new, tempestuous passion,
Of tenderness 'twill leave you not
The lingering and sweet impression.

But in an hour of agony,
Pray, speak it, and recall my image,
And say, "He still remembers me,
His heart alone still pays me homage."

1830

Demons

Spinning storm-clouds, rushing storm-clouds,
Hazy skies, a hazy night,
And a furtive moon that slyly
Sets the flying snow alight.
On we drive... The waste is boundless,
Nameless plains skim past, and hills.
Gripped by fear, I sit unmoving...
Tink-tink-tinkle go the bells.

"Coachman, come, wake up!.." "The horses
They are weary, sir, and slow;
As for me, I'm nearly blinded
By this blasted wind and snow!
There's no road in sight, so help me;
What to do?.. We've lost our way.
It's the demon that has got us
And is leading us astray.

"Look! He's close; he plays and teases,
Blows and spits, and, all unseen,
With a laugh our horses pushes
To the edge of a ravine.
Now he'll rise, a giant milepost,
Straight before me; now, a spark,
Flash and gleam, and, sinking, vanish
Of a sudden in the dark."

Spinning storm-clouds, rushing storm-clouds,
Hazy skies, a hazy night,
And a furtive moon that slyly
Sets the flying snow alight.
Spent from circling round, the horses
Jerk and stop... The bells go dead.
"That a stump or wolf?" "Yer Honour,
I don't rightly see ahead."

Loud the snow-storm weeps and rages,
And the horses snort in fright.
O'er the plain the demon prances,
In the murk his eyes glow bright.
Off the horses start a'shudder,
And the bells go ting-a-ling...
Demons, demons without number
Gather round us in a ring.

In the eerie play of moonlight
They grimace, they wail and call,
Whirling, leaping, dancing madly
Like the windswept leaves of fall.
Why are they so wild, so restless?
Why so weird the sounds they make?
Could this be a witch's wedding?
Could this be a goblin's wake?

Spinning storm-clouds, rushing storm-clouds,
Hazy skies, a hazy night,
And a furtive moon that slyly
Sets the flying snow alight.
Skyward soar the whirling demons,
Shrouded by the falling snow,
And their plaintive, awful howling
Fills my heart with dread and woe.

1830

Elegy

Of my mad years the vanished mirth and laughter
Affect me like a fume-filled morning-after.
Not so past pain—like wine is it to me
That as the years go by gains potency.
Sad is the path before me: toil and sorrow
Lie on the restless seaways of the morrow.

And yet from thought of death, my friends, I shrink;
I want to live—to suffer and to think,
And amid care and grief and tribulation,
Taste of sweet rapture and exhilaration;
Be drunk with harmony; touch fancy's strings
And freely weep o'er its imaginings...
And love's last flash, its smile of farewell tender
My sad decline may yet less mournful render.

1830

The Echo

When thunder beats its dreadful gong
Or wild beasts cry the woods among,
At sound of horn or maiden's song—
     Your answer clear
To every sound comes sharp and strong
     From empty air.

You hear the thunder's grinding shock
The roaring storm, the falling rock,
The shepherd calling to his flock
     And answer send
Receiving none again... Your lot—
     My poet friend!

1831

Autumn

AN EXCERPT

> Then does a host of thoughts
> my slumbering brain invade...
>
> *Derzhavin*

I

October has arrived; the grove the last remaining
Gold-speckled leaves sheds fast; the boughs hang brown
and bare;
A brook beyond the mill winds gay and uncomplaining,
But ice sheathes pond and road—a nip is in the air;
Off, eager, to the chase my neighbour rides, restraining
His chafing horse no more while horns expectant blare,
And by the boisterous sport the distant fields lie shaken,
And baying, hoarse-voiced packs the sleeping woods awaken.

II

'Tis autumn that I love; by spring am I laid low;
A thaw depresses me; I find my senses reeling,
A fever in my veins... The mud, the smells... A slow
Gloom on my heart descends... Contrariwise, how healing
Is winter with its frosts and sledge-rides o'er the snow,
Your love beside you, close, her trembling fingers stealing
Beneath the silky furs to curl around your own,
Their hot, their burning touch designed for you alone!

III

To don swift steel and glide o'er glassy streams—a merry
And pleasing way is this the wintry morn to spend!

Or else take winter's fêtes—how sparkling they, how very
Blithe and packed full of thrills! And yet confess, dear friend,
That e'en the sleepy bear would find it dull to bury
Himself amid the snows for half a year on end.
To sleigh-ride with young nymphs or by a fire sit moping—
That this won't pall in time is, I insist, past hoping!

IV

O beauteous summertime! I'd love you well without
The heat, the clouds of dust, the gnats and flies besetting
Mankind in buzzing swarms... Like fields we die of drought...
All our perceptions numbed, for lack of cool shade fretting
And of refreshing drink, we only think about
These simple needs, and winter's sure demise regretting,
The ancient dame send off with pancakes, and partake
Of quantities of ice and ices at her wake.

V

Late fall is viewed by most with unconcealed disfavour,
But I am spellbound held, dear readers, by its mild
And tranquil loveliness... No season is there braver,
More splendid in its way. Thus will an unloved child
My warm affections draw. Nay, friends, I do not waver
When I admit to it: my fancy is beguiled
By autumn's mellow charm. No vain or boastful lover,
The magic hid in it I waywardly discover.

VI

I love it as one might—how shall I best explain?—
Love a consumptive maid who, though too early fated
To die, meets her decline 'thout murmur, to complain
Unwilling... On her lips a smile still plays... Death's hated,
Grim visage is in sight, and yet her eye, 'tis plain,
Turns from his yawning jaws; he'll claim his long awaited,
Long sought-for prize, unseen... Her cheeks are flushed
                                                                and red...
Today she is alive, and on the morrow, dead.

VII

O drear and cheerless time, you charm the eye and tender
Contentment to the heart. How wondrous to behold
Your dying beauty is, the lush and sumptuous splendour
Of nature's farewell bloom: the forests clad in gold;
The wind's refreshing breath; the azure sky's surrender
To greyish, pearly haze; the pinch of early cold;
The fitful rays of sun that greet us for an instant,
And hoary winter's threats still undefined and distant.

VIII

When gracious autumn comes, my heart feels gay and light,
I am alive once more... Benign and salutary
Our Russian cold is, friends. My sleep, my appetite
It benefits, I vow. My very step grows airy;
The daily round of life brings me renewed delight;
Desires within me seethe... I'm young again and merry.
So am I built, so made, for which dull turns of speech
Your pardon, readers mine, herewith do I beseech.

IX

My horse is brought to me, and off he races, winging
Across the boundless wastes of open field and way.
Beneath his flashing hoofs the frozen ground is ringing
And cracking here and there... But brief's the light of day,
It wanes; and in the grate a fire is lighted, bringing
A cheery warmth with it... Drawn by the freakish play
Of leaping, darting flames, I loll nearby, perusing
A book, or, wrapped in thought, of many things sit musing.

X

Then, all the world forgot, in dulcet quietude
I fall beneath the spell of dulcet fancy's dreaming,
And poetry is born within me, and a mood
Of lyric restlessness o'erwhelms my spirit, seeming
To make it quiver, sing, and seek, no more subdued,

To pour out free at last and chainless... Toward me
                                            streaming,
Come callers by the score, upon me fast they gain;
Old friends they are of mine, the offspring of my brain.

XI

Thoughts flock to me in droves; they dance about and caper;
Swift rhymes to meet them rush; my fingers restive grow,
They boldly seek a pen; the pen, a sheet of paper...
A moment, and the verse will smoothly, freely flow.
So does a vessel doze till on her deck the dapper,
Quick-moving hands appear; up, down they creep, and lo! —
The winds fills out the sails, and, on her travels leaving,
The ship begins to move, the swelling waters cleaving.

XII

She's off!.. Where are we bound, for what mist-covered
                                            shores?..

. . . .
. . . .

1833

*   *   *

'Tis time, my friend, 'tis time! The heart to peace
                                aspires:
Day follows day; the rolling stream of hours
Crumbles the banks of being, and you and I
Had thought to live, and yet, behold, we die.

Though joy for ever flees, peace stays and
                                concentration.
For long now has it been my consolation,
Hard-driven slave, to plan rebellious flight
To some far sanctuary of work and chaste delight.

1834

Storm-Cloud

O storm-cloud, the tempest's survival, alone
Like mad do you rush o'er the heavenly dome;
Alone do you cast as you drift on your way
A dark, brooding shade on the jubilant day.

A short while ago you lay cloaking the sky,
And great forks of lightning flared round you on high.
You thundered and roared over forest and plain
And fed thirsting earth with a bounty of rain.

Enough! Make you haste! Do not tarry... Begone!
The earth is refreshed, and the rain-storm has flown,
And tame though the wind is, it stubbornly tries
To make you desert the now radiant skies.

1835

* * *

When, lost in thought, I wander from the town
And to the public cemetery come—
The railings, pillars, tombstones neat and pretty,
Beneath which rot the dead of all the city,
Packed side by side within the spongy sward
Like greedy guests about a sparse-set board,
The mausoleums of men of solid station,
The ugly ornament of third-rate masons,
And the inscriptions, graved in prose and verse,
Which all their virtues, service, ranks rehearse,
The doting cuckold marked by mourning cupids,
Pillars, robbed of their urns, forlornly fluted
Damp graves, awaiting with a weary yawn,
The tenants scheduled for tomorrow's morn—
I'm troubled by such thoughts of human folly
That I fall prey to spleen and melancholy
And want to spit and run...
                              Yet how I love
On autumn evenings, when the sky above
Sleeps like the dead in solemn quietude,
To walk in the ancestral solitude
Of our poor village graveyard, where there's space
For simple tombstones, and the thief's whey face
Does not intrude to rob when night is drear,
But the good villager a passing prayer
Murmurs, and sighs as he goes by these stones,
Ancient and plain, with lichen overgrown,
And, in the place of urns and pyramids
Of noseless Muses, unkempt caryatids,
An oak-tree spreads o'er venerable graves
And rustles fluttering leaves...

1836

4*

*   *   *

Exegi monumentum

A monument I've raised not built with hands,
And common folk shall keep the path well trodden
To where it unsubdued and towering stands
Higher than Alexander's Column.

I shall not wholly die—for in my sacred lyre
My spirit shall outlive my dust's corruption—
And honour shall I have, so long the glorious fire
Of poesy flames on one single scutcheon.

Rumour of me shall then my whole vast country fill,
In every tongue she owns my name she'll speak.
Proud Slave's posterity, Finn, and—unlettered still—
The Tungus, and the steppe-loving Kalmyk.

And long the people yet will honour me
Because my lyre was tuned to loving-kindness
And, in a cruel Age, I sang of Liberty
And mercy begged of Justice in her blindness.

Indifferent alike to praise or blame
Give heed, o Muse, but to the voice Divine
Fearing not injury, nor seeking fame,
Nor casting pearls to swine.

1836

NARRATIVE POEMS

The Gypsies

The Gypsies Bessarabia roam
In noisy crowds... Above a river
In tattered tents they make their home,
From night's cool breezes seeking cover.
In open air calm is their sleep;
Like freedom glad their rest is... Under
The rug-hung caravans there leap
A fire's bright flames whose shadows wander
And lick the wheels; close to the blaze,
A family, for supper gathered,
Prepare their meal; a tame bear lies
Behind the tent; nearby, untethered,
The horses graze... The steppe all round
Is full of life; their camping ground
The Gypsies leave at dawn; the ringing
Of anvils mingles with the sound
Of children's cries and women singing...
Then all at once a hush descends
Upon the camp; a horse's neighing
At times the dreamy quiet rends
Or else a watchdog's frantic baying.
To sleep the silent night is wed;
No lamp is on, no light aglimmer;
The moon sends down from overhead
A pearly-white, uncanny shimmer.
An old man, wakeful, by a tent
Sits, o'er a dying camp-fire bent,

The coals still warm; his absent gaze is
Fixed on the steppe, its vast extent
Embraced by night's thick, milky hazes...
His youthful daughter patiently
And dumbly he awaits: Zemphira
Is often out alone; no fear of
The wild's dark dangers haunts her; she
Loves freedom. But the arc, half-wasted,
Of moon for flight prepares; 'tis late,
And she does not appear... Untasted,
The old man's food cools on his plate.

Here is she now... Behind her trailing,
A man, a stranger comes. "I found
This man," she tells her father, hailing
Him cheerfully, "beyond the mound,
And that he was 'thout shelter seeing,
Invited him to share our tent.
He tells me he is well content
To be one of ourselves, a being
Free of all fetters. He will come,
Aleko will, where'er I take him.
He is an outlaw, Father. Make him,
I beg you, welcome in our home."

OLD MAN

I do so willingly. You may
With us till morn or longer stay,
'Tis as you wish... Your own forsaking,
Embrace our vagrant life and free,
And one of us, good youth, you'll be,
Of all we have in full partaking,
Though 'tis not much... At dawn we're making
Off in our caravan, and there
Is room in it for you. Choose any
Task, and it's yours, as is but fair:
Sing songs, forge metal, lead a bear
Round on a chain—our chores are many.

ALEKO

I'm joining you.

ZEMPHIRA

He's mine, and none
Can take him from me... But how sombre
The sky is. See—the moon has gone,
The steppe is haze-clad... Overcome
Am I, despite myself, by slumber...

———

Light dawns... The old man round the sleeping
Tent softly walks. "Zemphira, rise!
And you, my guest! The sun is creeping
Up from the hills. 'Tis time! The skies
Are bright. Come, leave your couch of languor!.."
The Gypsy folk rush noisily
From out their tents and fold them, eager
To load their caravans and be
Upon their way... They start, a sea
Of moving, heaving bodies, sprawling
Across the steppe and onward rolling:
Men, wives, young folk and old, a slow
Yet carefree crowd and gay and merry;
Beside their masters donkeys go
And crowing babes in baskets carry;
Noise, cries, a snatch of Gypsy song,
A bear's loud roar, his chain's dull clangour;
Women in gaudy rags, a brood
Of children barefoot and half-nude;
Dogs giving tongue in sudden anger;
The creak of wagon wheels, the whine
Of bagpipes... All is in commotion,
In discord wild, but full of motion
And life, unlike our own supine
And idle ways, as dead and weary
As are the songs of bondsmen dreary!..

———

Aleko gazed upon the plain,
A secret grief his spirit chilling.
Whence came it he was little willing,
Nay, more, he dreaded to explain.

He had a mate, black-eyed Zemphira,
And he was free, and there were clearer
Skies o'er him now, lit by a sun
Of southern lavishness and splendour.
Why then did he to gloom surrender?
By what dark care was he o'ercome?

Happy bird that roams the lonely
Span of sky, its bright blue dome!
For a summer's sojourn only
Do you build your fragile home.
On a bough in wood or clearing
You sit dozing all night long,
And of morn, God's summons hearing,
Greet the radiant sun with song.
After beauteous springtime's passing
And hot summer's sad demise
Autumn comes, grey clouds amassing
In the dismal, foggy skies.
Dull of heart we turn and weary...
Happy bird! For swift you wing
'Cross the seas, in blithe and cheery
Southern climes to dwell till spring.

A carefree bird of passage, flying
To shores far from his homeland lying,
Our exile was. No nest had he;
To follow any road felt free;
Of no one place grew fond; wherever
Night overtook him, he would sleep,
Each new-born day into the keep
Of Heaven giving. Nor was ever
His idling heart touched by the fever
And pulse of life, though sometimes deep
Within it stirred the lure of distant,
Of magical and taunting fame
And though sweet visions for an instant
To him of sumptuous revels came.
He minded not the roar of thunder
And oft serenely dozing lay
'Neath murky, rainy skies or under
The morning sun's warm, playful ray.

Of blind and crafty fate denying
The power, he faced it unafraid.
But, O, dear God, his will defying,
How with his heart the passions played!
They seethed within him, and his shaken
And tortured soul left ne'er alone.
Suppressed, contained, they will awaken—
When? Wait and see... I doubt not, soon!

ZEMPHIRA

Say, love: the things you left behind you,
Do you not miss them?

ALEKO

                Tell me, pray:
What did I leave?

ZEMPHIRA

         Need I remind you?—
Your land, your towns and people.

ALEKO

             Nay.
I'm free of them and do not rue it.
There's naught to miss, if but you knew it.
Our towns are stifling cloisters where
Spring's fragrant breezes never carry
From flowery meadowlands and nary
A breath will reach of fresh, cool air;
Where love is scorned, like all true feeling,
Thought hunted down and freedom sold,
Where men, before their idols kneeling,
Plead shamelessly for chains and gold.
What left I there?—Betrayal and worry,
Of prejudice the damning word,
Disgrace attired in robes of glory,
The persecution of the herd!

ZEMPHIRA

And glittering halls, and tables laden
With food and drink, much noise and light,
Games, feasts and balls, the faces bright
Of richly garbed, bejewelled maidens.

ALEKO

Where love is not, mirth is unknown
And life is stale and holds no relish.
As for the maids, as lifeless stone
Their beauty is beside your own
Which no rich gems or pearls embellish.
Be as you are, I beg, change not!..
My one desire but now discovered
Is that you share an exile's lot
And fortunes with him, my beloved.

OLD MAN

I know you like us not the less
Though born you were to wealth and leisure,
But freedom he the less might treasure
Whose youth was spent in idleness.
A legend that has never vanished
But lives among us, speaks of one
Who by his emperor was banished
From southern parts. His name is gone
From me, but that 'twas here he languished,
This I recall... Though well along
In years he was, yet young of spirit
And with the gift divine of song
Endowed from birth; his voice—to hear it
Was as to hear the murmur of
A mountain stream... By fate transplanted
Onto these shores, he drew the love
Of all and with his verse enchanted
The hearts of men. A very child
The bard by nature was; his neighbours
Helped the man fish and snare what wild
Game he might need, and thus his labours
The lighter made. In winter, when

Ice bound the stream and winds howled, raging,
In fur skins did they clothe the aging
Songsmith, a saint among mere men.
But to a life so mean and stinted
He could, alas, but ill adjust,
And daily weaker grew, and hinted
At Heaven's wrath and said 'twas just,
That for his sins he now was paying...
For sweet deliverance fervent praying,
Along the Danube shores, an old
And broken man, he sadly wandered
And, weeping bitter tears, recalled
His own dear land... Her fates he pondered
Until the last; and, lying on
His deathbed, asked, his strength fast waning,
That his remains be southward borne,
The shores from which he had been torn
Even in death his spirit claiming!

ALEKO

Such is thy children's destiny,
O Rome, thou great and lustrous city!..
What's wordly fame?.. Come, answer me,
Bard of the gods, of love and beauty—
A fleeting word of praise, the cold
And dull lament of church-bells ringing
Verse, deathless through the ages winging
Or else a tale by Gypsies told?..

Two summers pass, fast onward winding,
And still the steppe the Gypsies roam,
Where'er their pathways take them, finding
A ready welcome and a home.
Civilisation's fetters spurning,
Aleko is as free as they.
In him the past excites no yearning:
A nomad he, and one will stay.
Zemphira's with him and her father;
Their life is his, he can no other
Recall: he loves the Gypsy ways,

Their poor but tuneful tongue, the glowing
Nights 'neath the stars, the swiftly flowing,
Yet indolent and blissful days.
With them where'er they go they carry
A beast, fierce dweller of a lair.
Watched by a crowd that gathers, wary,
Beside a village inn, the bear
Stamps, dancing, up and down, and, seeming
To weary from't, gnaws at his chain
And loudly roars now and again.
The old man on his staff stands leaning
And beating lazily upon
A tambourine. Aleko, singing
A song, his charge leads round. With swinging
Skirts comes Zemphira; one by one
The proffered coins she takes... For supper
They cook some millet; then, sweet sleep
In tent, now darkened, takes the upper
Hand, and till morn the hush reigns deep.

———————

The aged Gypsy warms his aching
Bones in the sun; o'er cradle bent,
His daughter sings; in wonderment
Aleko lists, his anger waking.

ZEMPHIRA

Husband mine, old and stern,
Stab your wife, kill your wife!
Naught will stop me, for I
Have no fear of your knife.

Husband mine, old and scorned,
Love another I do.
I will love unto death,
But not you, but not you.

ALEKO

Hush... Sing your song no more, I pray you!
I loathe its odd and savage ring.

ZEMPHIRA

Indeed! Think you I will obey you?
'Tis for myself, not you I sing.
Husband mine, old and stern,
Stab me, cast me in flame.
Know: whatever you do,
I'll not tell you his name.

He is young, he is bold,
I am under his spell.
Fresh as springtime is he,
And he loves me full well.

We embraced and we kissed,
In the quiet of night.
How we laughed, husband mine,
When we thought of your plight.

ALEKO

Stop, wife! All's well, let us forget it...

ZEMPHIRA

My song—think you it rings not true?

ALEKO

Zemphira!

ZEMPHIRA

                    Ha! You will not let it
Provoke you? Strange! ... I sang of you.

Walks off, singing: "Husband mine...", etc.

OLD MAN

I know the song—it is a pleasing
And lightsome piece. When I was young,
The ear of all who heard it teasing,

'Twas, I remember, often sung.
On winter days, to our young daughter
My Mariula, sitting by
A fire (how beautiful I thought her!),
Would sing it for a lullaby.
As time goes on the past grows dimmer
Till but a shred is left to me.
But this old song remains for ever
Engraved upon my memory.

———

All's still. The southern sky is lighted
By moon's soft glow, its ray nigh white.
Zemphira, waking in the night,
Her parent rouses: "I am frighted—
Look at Aleko, Father. He
Groans in his sleep most horribly."

OLD MAN

Disturb him not, for when a sleeping
Man moans and gasps and tosses, weeping,
Upon his bed, it means, so say
The Russians, that a spirit's keeping
Him choked and breathless. 'Twill away,
Not to return, at breath of day.

ZEMPHIRA

Yet whispers he my name, Zemphira.

OLD MAN

He seeks for you in sleep. Than all
The world to him you, child, are dearer.

ZEMPHIRA

His love that held me once in thrall
Now wearies me. 'Tis freedom, Father,
My heart desires... But hark! Again
A name he speaks—not mine, another...

OLD MAN

Whose name?

ZEMPHIRA
He grits his teeth, of pain
A moan escapes him... I shall wake him,
'Tis fearful.

OLD MAN

Stay! 'Twill soon forsake him,
The nightly spirit will. Keep calm,
I pray you, child.

ZEMPHIRA

Do not you hear him?
He calls to me, I must be near him,
Else, Father, might he come to harm.

ALEKO

Where were you?

ZEMPHIRA

I? With father, yonder.
You seemed to be harassed by some
Dark spirit that nigh tore asunder
Your very soul. By fear o'ercome
Was I. Your teeth in anguish grinding,
You called my name.

ALEKO

I dreamed of you.
Black were those dreams... My vision
                              blinding,
Some evil shape stood 'twixt us two.

ZEMPHIRA

Why trust in dreams?

ALEKO

I swear to Heaven,
There's naught I trust! Alas, 'tis so—
Not dreams, not words and vows, not even
Your heart, my wife, if you must know.

OLD MAN

Why, youthful madman, do you sigh?
Here men are free, and tempers mellow,
And women lovely, and the yellow
Sun shines undimmed in azure sky.
Succumb to gloom, and you will perish.

ALEKO

She loves me not whose love I cherish.

OLD MAN

Be comforted: a child is she.
'Tis folly to give way to sadness:
You love with bitter, aching madness;
A woman's heart loves jestingly.
Look overhead where stretch the soaring
Plains of the sky and watch the slight
Disc of the moon glide o'er them, pouring
Upon the earth its steady light.
'Twill with a cloud spend moments fleeting
And bathe it in its dazzling ray,
Then leave it, and, another meeting,
Illumine it and drift away.
To chain a maiden's heart by saying,
"Be faithful to a single love,"
Is as to keep the moon from straying
Over the lone expanse above...
Grieve not.

ALEKO

She loved me!.. O'er me kneeling,
She passed the lonely hours of night,

With open gladness and delight
Her tenderness and love revealing!..
Full of a childish gaiety,
How oft with sweet and guileless chatter
Or rapturous kisses did she scatter
My darksome thoughts and drive from me
The gloom that would at times invade me!..
And now ... my own Zemphira, she
Who loved me so, *she* has betrayed me!

OLD MAN

Come, hark to me and listen well:
Of my own self a tale I'll tell.
It happened long ago, Aleko,
When Moscow held no threat for us—
(These words of mine contain an echo
Of times and matters ominous).
The sultan then we stood in fear of;
Ensconced in lofty Ackerman,
A pasha ruled Budjak... Now hear of
Less awesome things. I was a man
Young, full of life, and overflowing
With spirits gay; my locks were black,
No silver thread among them showing...
Of lovely maids we had no lack,
But there was one—e'en to behold her
Was bliss—I loved her from afar...
Then came a day—my own I called her.

As swiftly as a shooting star
Youth flashes past, but love grows cooler
And passes faster still, a ruler
Whose reign is brief: for but one year
Held I the love of Mariula.

Once, when we'd set our tents up near
Kagul, there joined us of an evening
An alien tribe of Gypsies. They
Made camp nearby and there did stay
For two short nights, the camp-site leaving
By stealth just as the third came round.
With them without a word of sound

My Mariula went, forsaking
Her sleeping child. At dawn awaking,
I found her gone... In vain did I
Search for her endlessly and cry
Her name—she'd vanished... I was stricken...
Zemphira wailed; with her I wept.
E'er since the thought of love would sicken
And irk me; to myself I kept
The more as time went on, refusing
All offers of a mate and choosing
To live alone these many years.

ALEKO

Why did you not pursue the fierce
Beast and your wife, that sweet deceiver,
And, moved by passion's blinding fever,
Their hearts with vengeful dagger pierce?

OLD MAN

Freer than a bird is love: endeavour
To cage it, and from you 'twill fly.
It comes, and then, alas, for ever
It goes, however much you try
To keep it...

ALEKO

What?! From vengeance shying,
To cede what is your own by right?
Nay, never!.. For a wrong or slight
Pay back in full I would... If, lying
Above the sea, my rival I
Found on a shelf of rock, then, by
The gods I swear, that I'd not leave him
To sleep there peacefully, but heave him,
Defenceless though the villain be,
Over the edge, and roar with laughter
In doing so, o'erjoyed to see
His fear, and for a long time after
At thought of it be filled with glee.

YOUNG GYPSY

One more caress... Be you not chary
Of kisses, wench.

ZEMPHIRA

My husband is
A jealous man and bitter. Tarry
I dare not...

YOUNG GYPSY

Wait! One last, sweet kiss...
When do we meet?

ZEMPHIRA

We must be wary.
I'll see you when the moon has set,
Beyond the mound.

YOUNG GYPSY

You'll not deceive me?
You'll come?

ZEMPHIRA

Go now and do not fret.
I will be there, dear heart, believe me.

———

Aleko sleeps and in his dream
He is pursued by blurred and fleeting
But frightful visions. With a scream
He starts awake, and gropes with beating
Heart for his mate... His faltering hand
Encounters tumbled sheets, but, meeting
Naught else, hangs limp... He rises and
Looks round... The hush about him reigning
Tells him the worst... No more restraining

His rising fears, he goes now cold,
Now hot, by turn, and blindly stumbles
Outside... All's dark... The steppeland slumbers
About him... Strands of mist enfold
A furtive moon... Around the sleeping
Camp-site with visage pale and grim
He prowls alone... The stars shine dim,
Their wavering light, through cloud banks seeping,
Discovers tracks... Across the lea
He follows them impatiently.

A grave beside the roadway showing,
White in the dark, now draws his gaze.
With sick foreboding filled, his slowing
Steps, in a kind of trance or daze,
He thither drags... His lips are shaking
And, too, his knees... Ahead there loom
Two shades, two figures... Toward them making,
He hears them whisper in the gloom,
Above the sullied stone...

FIRST VOICE

                         Nay, truly,
I must away...

SECOND VOICE

             Would you thus coolly
Leave me and go? Wait until day.

FIRST VOICE

I mayn't. 'Tis trouble you are wooing.

SECOND VOICE

Your love is shy.

FIRST VOICE

                Of my undoing
You'll be the tool...

SECOND VOICE

Go not, I pray.

FIRST VOICE

What if my husband wakens?

ALEKO

Stay!
He has awakened and salutes you.
Bide here, I beg, this graveside suits you.

ZEMPHIRA

Run, love!..

ALEKO

Why haste you to be gone?
Be not so quick, my handsome one.
Lie still!

Stabs him with a knife.

ZEMPHIRA

Aleko!

GYPSY

I am dying...

ZEMPHIRA

You've killed him!.. Look! His blood's upon
Your hands... You meant for him to perish,
I know it!..

ALEKO

What is done is done.
Now in his love can you take relish.

ZEMPHIRA

You ghoul, you ruthless villain! I
Who loved you once despise and scorn you
And curse the demon who has borne you!..

ALEKO

Die then!

Stabs her.

ZEMPHIRA

With love for him I die...

———

The dawn-lit East shone bright... Still holding
His knife, upon the grave's cold stone,
The steppe before him calm unfolding,
Aleko, dark of face, sat lone
And motionless, his clothing bloody,
And at his feet stretched out, his own
Zemphira lifeless lay, her body
Beside her lover's... Round them milled
The Gypsies, troubled they and fearful.
One after one, their women, chilled
By sorrow, o'er the dead bent, tearful,
And gently kissed the sightless eyes.
Zemphira's father, paralysed
With grief, watched as the two were carried
To where the new-dug grave did lie
In wait for them and where, slain by
One hand, they now were placed and buried...
Aleko from afar looked on,
And when of earth the final handful
The bodies hid, he toppled down
From off the stone, his senses reeling,
And lay there void of thought and feeling...

The old man then drew near and said:
"Go, proud one, leave us! We are led

By different laws and want among us
No murderer... Go where you will!
By your black deeds and foul you wrong us
Who do not like to wound or kill.
Your love of freedom—how you flaunt it!
Yet for yourself alone you want it,
This freedom, and a stranger dwell
Here in our midst. We're kind and humble;
You're hard; where you dare tread, we stumble—
So go in peace and fare you well."

This said he, and with noise and rumble
Of wheels the Gypsy camp was soon
Upon its way, the scene deserting
Of nightly horror and of doom.
'Fore long, the fateful valley skirting,
The caravan was lost to sight...
O'erhung by rugs whose tints, once bright,
Had dulled, a van still stood forlornly
Out in the steppe... So on a lonely
And misty dawn, with winter near,
A flight of cranes will leave the drear
Fields and with shrill and piercing clamour
Fly south, not to return till summer,
Their badly wounded, trembling mate
Abandoning to cruel fate...
Dusk came, then dark; the van, benighted,
Stood lone and empty; no man kept
Vigil beside it, near it lighted
A fire, or 'neath its rooftop slept.

EPILOGUE

So out the past, time's passage scorning,
The magic wand of poesy
Now days of joy, now days of mourning
Evokes and brings to life for me.

In parts where battles once roared unending
And where the limits of its rule
The Russians, with the Turks contending,

Triumphant, showed to Istanbul,
Where still our old, two-headed eagle
Of glories past the mantle regal
Wears, in the steppeland, once the seat
Of vanished clans and war-camps ancient,
The gay-voiced Gypsies, tramping patient
Down dusty roadways, I did meet.
They freedom loved and peace, and, roaming
The steppe with them, their simple fare
And simple life I liked to share,
And 'fore their camp-fires, in the gloaming,
Dozed off and found such slumber sweet.
Their merry songs my heart was full of
And oft the name of Mariula
With tenderness did I repeat.

And yet, O nature's children, nurtured
And reared in want, you, too, like we,
By dreaded dreams and visions tortured,
Know little of true felicity.
In those poor, makeshift tents you fashion
From troublous life you cannot flee.
There's no defence from fatal passion
And no escape from destiny.

1824

The Bronze Horseman

A Tale of St. Petersburg

FOREWORD

The incident here described is based on fact.
Particulars relating to the flood have been
borrowed from contemporary publications.
The curious can compare them with the
account left by V. N. Bergh.

INTRODUCTION

Where lonely waters, struggling, sought
To reach the sea, *he* paused, in thought
Immersed, and gazed ahead. The river
Swept grandly past. In midstream caught,
A peeling bark did bounce and shiver
Upon the waves. And here and there,
On moss-grown, boggy shores a rare,
Ramshackle hut loomed dark, the dwelling
Of humble Finn... The sun's bright glare
In milky fog was shrouded; falling
On forests dense, its sickly ray
Ne'er pierced their murk.

              Thought he: the haughty
Swede here we'll curb and hold at bay
And here, to gall him, found a city.
As nature bids so must we do:
A window will we cut here through
On Europe, and a foothold gaining
Upon this coast, the ships we'll hail
Of every flag, and freely sail
These seas, no more ourselves restraining.

A century passed, and there it stood,
Of Northern lands the pride and beauty,
A young, resplendent, gracious city,
Sprung out the dark of mire and wood.
Where Finnish fisherman, forlorn
Stepchild of Fortune, came, disturbing
The peace and calm, to cast his worn,
Much mended net into the turbid,
Mysterious waters, now there rise
Great palaces and towers; a maze
Of sails and mastheads crowds the harbour;
Ships of all ports moor here beside
These rich and peopled shores; the wide,
Majestic Neva slowly labours,
In granite clad, to push its way
'Neath graceful bridges; gardens cover
The once bare isles that dot the river,
Its glassy surface calm and grey.
Old Moscow fades beside her rival:
A dowager, she is outshone,
O'ershadowed by the new arrival,
Who, robed in purple, mounts the throne.

I love thee, Peter's proud creation,
Thy princely stateliness of line,
The regal Neva coursing patient
'Twixt sober walls of massive stone;
The iron lacework of thy fences,
Thy wistful, moonless, lustrous nights,
Dusk-clothed but limpid... Oft it chances
That in my chamber 'thout a light
I write or sit a book perusing
Whilst, luminous, the streets lie dozing
Beyond great, empty blocks... Up higher,
'Gainst sky, the Admiralty spire
Is clearly etched...
                    The darkness driving
From off the heavens, twilight hastes
To welcome twilight, scarcely giving
Night half an hour...
                    I love thy chaste,
Inclement winter with its bracing
And moveless air, the lusty bite

And pinch of frost, the sledges racing
On Neva banks, the bloom of bright
Young cheeks, the ballroom's noise and glitter,
And, at a bachelors' get-together,
The hiss and sparkle of iced champagne
And punch bowls topped with bluish flame.
I love the dash and animation
Of Fields of Mars where, trim and staid,
Both foot and horse pass on parade,
Their symmetry and neat formation
A pretty sight. In battles charred,
Here flags sail by, triumphant flowing,
There helmets meet the eye, their glowing,
Well furbished sides by bullets scarred.
I love to hear the thunder crashing,
O gallant city mine and fair,
When to the royal house of Russia
The tsar's young spouse presents an heir;
When mark we, full of pride and glee,
Our latest martial victory,
Or when the Neva boldly smashes
Its pale-blue chains, and off to sea
The crumbling ice exultant rushes.

Stand thou, O Peter's citadel,
Like Russia steadfast and enduring,
And let the elements rebel
No more but be subdued; your fury
Contain, O Finnish waves, and quell,
Forget the old feud and endeavour
To let it buried stay forever,
And undisturbed leave Peter's sleep!..

Fresh in our memories we keep
A time most grim and dark and baneful...
Upon my narrative with dread
Do I embark—the task is painful,
Grave, friends, it needs must be and sad.

PART ONE

Chilled by the breath of bleak November,
The city dismal lay and sombre...

'Gainst granite banks its waves of lead
With plashing sound a restless Neva
Flung wildly as it fidgeted
And tossed like one abed with fever.
The hour was late: 'twas dark; the rain
Beat angrily against the pane;
The wind howled plaintively, unceasing...
'Twas then that young Yevgeny came
Home from a party. By that name
Our hero will we call. 'Tis pleasing,
And suits him well enough, and then
It has been friendly with my pen
For many a year. Nor have we any
Need of a surname: our Yevgeny
Can do without. Although of yore
It might have shone and been accorded
A worthy place in Russian lore,
Though Karamzín might have recorded
Its fame, today 'tis mentioned not
And is by all the world forgot...
A clerk and in Kolómna living,
Our hero shunned the gentry, giving
No thought, of proud ambition free,
To his illustrious ancestry.

And so, once in his house, Yevgeny
Shook out his rain-soaked cloak, undressed
And went to bed. He tried his best
To go to sleep, but failed: too many
Thoughts filled his brain. That he was poor,
Of this he mused; that to secure
A post was hard; that on his labours
His prospects hung and livelihood;
That wealth and wit and suchlike favours
Of God he was denied; that wooed
By Fortune were the least deserving
And worthy; that he'd now been serving
As office clerk for nigh on two
Whole years; that—look you now—the weather
Was turning nasty altogether;
That, as the river level grew,
The bridges would be raised above it,
Which meant that he and his beloved

Parasha might be parted for
A day or two, or even more.

He sighed, and, like a true-born poet,
Lost in a dream, let fancy roam:
"Why not get married, have a home,
A family?.. In fact, I owe it
To both of us... Things won't be bad,
Though hard at first—I'm young, and glad
To toil 'thout respite, all else brushing
Aside... I'll build us two a nest,
A modest one, and there Parasha
Install... In time, a year, at best,
Once I've secured a post and station,
To her will go the education
And rearing of our progeny...
With spirit calm life's storms
                    we'll weather,
And buried at its end together
Will by our children's children be..."

Such were his thoughts. Yet low of spirit
He was, and wished the wind would moan
A sight less mournfully, to hear it
Depressed one so, and that the rain
Were not so drear, so persevering...
He slept at last... And now the haze
Of night thinned out, fast disappearing...
And o'er the town pale day did rise...
A fearful day!
               Throughout the night
The frenzied Neva had insanely
The storm been charging, trying vainly
To gain the sea, the tempest's might
Its efforts foiling...
              In the morning
Crowds came to watch the rising domes
Of waves that, all defences scorning,
Lashed at the banks with spray and foam.
Barred from the bay by wind, the Neva
Turned, chafing, back, and with a roar,
By savage wrath and passion driven,
The islands flooded... Ever more

Fierce grew the storm. The river, raving,
Did seethe and boil and fume and swell,
And like a beast, for vengeance craving,
Enraged, upon the city fell.
All fled before it; streets were emptied;
Canals rose high and overflowed;
Swift torrents into basements flowed
And cellars and, audacious, raided
The homes and warerooms they invaded...
The city, to the waist submerged,
Like Triton from the floods emerged.

A siege! An onslaught! Onward sweeping,
The waves advance, like robbers creeping
In through the windows, broken by
Boats flailed by wind... Where'er the eye
Can reach, a host of things comes drifting:
Logs, roofing, stalls, the wares of thrifty
Tradesmen, a bridge and furniture,
The prized belongings of the poor,
Huts, coffins from a graveyard...
                                        Stricken
By God's unlooked-for, awful wrath,
The people wait for certain death!..
No food, no shelter... Doomed to sicken
Are they and perish all...
                                    The late
And reverenced tsar the scepter wielded
Of Russia then, and grief so great
Was his that, burdened by its weight,
He said: "Not e'en a prince is shielded
From God's displeasure, for is he
Before the elements defenceless..."
And standing on his balcony,
He watched with pensive eye the senseless
And dire destruction wrought... The square
Was one vast lake and everywhere
The streets were streams; with seeming malice
They toward it rushed as if to snare
The lonely isle that was the palace...
The sovereign spoke—his generals brave,
'Cross deluged streets before them lying,

At once set forth, the floods defying,
The drowning, fear-crazed folk to save.

On Peter's square where, built but lately,
A mansion stood, most rich and stately,
Beside whose entrance lions two
Rose lifelike, huge, their paws uplifted,
Yevgeny who had somehow drifted
To this fine neighbourhood and who
Was hatless, with his face the hue
Of death, immobile sat and quiet
Astride a marble beast... The riot
Of angry waves that raged below
He noticed not; it was as though
He did not see them upward rearing
And avid, hungry, lick his heels,
Nor hear the howling wind that, veering,
Had snatched his hat away, nor feel
The rain lash at his face... Despairing,
He stared ahead where mountain-high
The dreaded billows rose, ensnaring
All in their path, where, shattered by
The tempest, bits of wreckage floated...
'Twas not his safety, be it noted,
Our poor Yevgeny feared for—nay,
Far from't... There stood beside the bay
A cottage by a willow shaded,
A tiny place, behind a faded
And crooked fence, and in it his
Parasha and her widowed mother
Lived all alone... Oh, God! Is this
A dream or is our life another
Of Heaven's jests at man's expense,
A fantasy, a nothingness?..

Like one bewitched and chained, a being
Lost to the world, he sits there, seeing
Naught but the water round him, and
Is powerless to move or stand!
And high above him, all undaunted
By foaming stream and flooded shores,
Deaf to the storm's rebellious roars,
With hand outstretched, the Idol, mounted
On steed of bronze, majestic, soars.

PART TWO

At last, with wild destruction sated
And worn with so much violence,
Its thirst and fury now abated,
No more the Neva hesitated
But with a studied negligence
Decamped, its plunder shedding. So
A brigand and his band of low
Cutthroats and thieves into a village
Might break, and there maraud and pillage,
And shout, and curse, and smash, and shoot
Till, spent at last and nigh prostrated,
They fly, their confidence deflated
By fear of capture, of their loot
The greater part behind them leaving...

The water sank, and this perceiving,
Yevgeny hastened, quick of foot.
The sight he saw but half believing,
At once by hope and anguish led,
To where the river in its bed
Still seethed, by victory elated,
Its anger fierce, unmitigated.
As if by smouldering fires fed,
Still fumed, and tossed, and wept, and ranted,
Still foamed and like a charger panted
From field of combat newly fled...
Yevgeny now a skiff espying,
He hurries, for the boatman crying,
To where 'tis moored. Ten copeks serve:
To carry him across agreeing,
The man takes charge in earnest, being
Not one to lightly lose his nerve.

Long did the practiced boatman follow
That risky course and ply his oars,
Oft were the waves about to swallow
The boat as flung into a hollow
Between two crests it was, before
The shore was reached.
                              In awe and terror
Yevgeny gazed about him, for

These streets he knew so well now bore
An unfamiliar look... What error
Was this?.. Destruction all around:
Some houses levelled were with the ground,
Some bent, their doors and windows shattered,
Some moved from place; nearby, lay scattered,
As on a battlefield, the dead...
Half-crazed, Yevgeny ran ahead,
The streets he traversed noting dimly,
Oblivious of all except
His torment, to the place where grimly,
As with a sealed-up letter kept
For him to open, Fate awaited
With tidings better left concealed...
Here was the suburb now. With bated
Breath did he stop to look. Revealed
To sight, the bay stretched grey and lonely.
Her house, he knew, stood near it... Only
Where was it? Where?..

          He moved away,
Then stumbled back in stark dismay.
This was the spot, a willow growing
Nearby... Had house and fence been borne
Away by floods?.. He walked with slowing
Steps all around... Wild words were torn
From him in spasms, by fits of laughter
Succeeded...

        'Twas a good time after
That like a shroud night's haze upon
The weary city fell. Not one
Amongst its dwellers slept, however.
Instead, in talk did they endeavour
To ease their hearts, that troublous day
Discussing...

        When bright morning's ray
From out the pallid clouds came stealing,
Of ruin it found but little trace,
The crimson robes of dawn concealing
The ravages of yesterday.
Life was resumed and went its way
In peace again. The townsfolk hurried,
As unconcerned and little worried
As ever, down the streets. Astir

At early hour the hucksters were
And office clerks. The former, chastened
But firm, to open storerooms by
The Neva robbed did fairly fly
And at expense of shoppers hastened
To make their losses good.
                                        Khvostóv,
A count and bard beloved of
The gods, in deathless verse and ringing
Already of the trials was singing
By Peter's city suffered.
                                        As
For poor Yevgeny, more's the pity,
His muddled brain succumbed, alas,
To shock and grief. Alone the city
For days he prowled, and in his ear
The roar of wind and Neva sounded.
Tormented by a nameless fear
And crushing thought he was, and hounded
By fitful dreams. Weeks came and went,
A month, and still without intent
He stalked the streets. A gloom surrounded
And hemmed him in. He did not go
Back to his rooms again, and to
A poor young poet they were rented.
Nor did he ever think to call
For his belongings but contented
Himself with what he wore. To all
The world he soon became a stranger...
By day, he tramped about; at night,
Slept on the wharf. A sorry sight
He was, his clothes in rags, and eating
The morsels pity thrust into
His hand. A brood of urchins meeting,
He pelted was with stones, and, too,
Was often stung with whips, as, seeing
The passing coaches not, he crossed
The roads, to all about him lost,
Stunned, deafened by his pain, yet fleeing,
Unconscious, from't... And thus did he
His days drag out in agony,
No man, no beast, no phantom, truly,
And yet no living soul...

One day,
The transient summer ceding duly
To autumn, fast asleep he lay
Beside the quay... The Neva's grey
Waves whined and sobbed, a plaint repeating
And 'gainst the steps in anguish beating
Like a petitioner at door
Of hardened judges who ignore
His plea...
    Yevgeny woke, and dreary
The scene about him was: a weary
Rain fell in drops, the wind of fall
Howled, and a sentry's distant call
Came in reply, the darkness rending...
He rose in haste, not comprehending
Where 'twas he found himself, and yet,
By horrors past his mind beset,
Seeing them clearly... Off he staggered,
Then stopped, his eye with terror glazed,
His countenance grown dark and haggard,
For what he saw left him full dazed:
There, 'fore him stood a pillared mansion,
And two stone lions to attention
Rose on its porch and flanked the door,
While 'bove the rock, by chains defended,
The fearsome Idol, hand extended,
On steed of bronze did proudly soar.

Yevgeny shivered. Anew there bound him
The old, consuming, cruel pain.
With lucid mind he saw again
The waves, rapacious, press around him
And hiss and roar in spite. He knew
The square, the house, the lions two,
And him who towered, by murk surrounded,
Above them all, detached and still,
One who, Fate bowing to his will,
The city on the sea had founded...
Enclosed by night, how fearful he!
How deeply plunged in revery!
In him what dreaded force is hidden!
His horse, what fire is in its eye!
Where dost thou, steed, in frenzy fly

And where to halt wilt thou be bidden?..
'Twas thus, O sovereign great and steer
Of Fate, the captain of her choosing,
That Rus, a bridle of iron using,
Above the chasm you forced to rear!

Around the pedestal, dejected,
Poor, sick Yevgeny made his way,
His gaze on him who had in sway
Held half the world, in awe directed.
His chest felt tight. Against a grille
He pressed his burning face, but still
His blood flamed and his heart went racing
And pounding madly... Weak of limb,
Wild-eyed, his fingers clenched, the grim
And haughty Idol sullen facing,
Like one possessed, he, trembling, stood,
And in a quivering voice and breaking
Brought faintly out, with fury shaking,
"Good, thou most wondrous builder, good!
Just wait and see!.." 'Twas all he could
Give utterance to, but stopped, and stricken
With terror, turned and fled: the tsar
Was eyeing him... That wrathful stare
That never left him, made him quicken
His steps. Across the empty square
Yevgeny ran and seemed to hear
Great, swelling, mighty peals of thunder,
And feel the pavement quaking under
A horse's heavy hoofs. For there,
Behind him, to the darkness wedded,
Lit by the moon's pale ray and slight,
One hand in warning raised, the dreaded
Bronze Horseman galloped through the night.
Till morn, where'er Yevgeny, frighted,
Did bend his steps and wander, mute,
The fell Bronze Horseman rode, benighted,
In mad, in thunderous pursuit.

And ever since, when, little knowing
Where 'twas he went, he chanced to cross
That square, confused and restless growing,
He'd stand there, cowed and at a loss,

And to his heart his hand press quickly
To still the pain within, a sickly
Look on his face; then in dismay
Removed his cap and slink away,
Nor once look up...
                    A lonely island
Lies off the coast. At end of day
A tardy fisherman his way
Might there make in his boat, and, silent,
His scanty supper on the shore
Cook in the dusk of evening, or
A clerk might choose it for an outing
On Sabbath day. The isle is bare
Of shrubbery, no grasses sprouting
Upon its soil. The flood did there
A cottage bring that perched, forsaken,
Above the water like a dark,
Misshapen stump till spring, when taken
Away it was. The ugly mark
It bore of waves that had, unhurried,
Wrought its destruction and decay...
Beside it, dead, my madman lay,
And there, so God willed, he was buried.

1833

DRAMAS

The Covetous Knight

Scenes from the tragicomedy by Shenstone.

SCENE I

In a tower.
ALBERT and IVAN.

ALBERT

I care not what it costs me, at the tourney
Appear I shall. Show me my helmet, Ivan.

IVAN brings him the helmet.

'Tis cleft and broken and for wear unfit.
I needs must have a new one. What a blow
He struck me, that young villain, Count Delorge!

IVAN

You paid him back in kind, sir: from his stirrups
He fairly flew, and for a day and night
Lay senseless, 'thout a sign or breath of life.

ALBERT

Yet 'tis not he, I vow, who's out of pocket,
For his Venetian breastplate is unscathed.
As for his breast, 'twon't cost the man a copper:
From purchasing a new one he'll desist.
Why did I not upon the spot remove

His helmet?.. Fie!.. 'Twas shame that held me back,
The ladies being present and the Duke.
A curse upon the count! Why could not he
Have cracked my skull!.. In need of new apparel
Am I beside. At table were all the knights
Attired in silk and velvet; I alone
Wore mail and had to plead that it was chance
Had brought me to the tourney. In excuse
What will I say today? O poverty!
How you debase the heart and crush the spirit!
When Count Delorge with his great, heavy lance
My helmet pierced and flung it to the ground
And galloped past, and I with head uncovered
Set spurs to my Emir and like a whirlwind
Went after him and sent the good count flying
Nigh twenty paces, like as though he were
A puny page; when all the ladies rose
And e'en Clotilde could not suppress a cry;
When heralds hailed my prowess—none divined
By what this fine display of matchless strength
And courage had been prompted; none could know
That I had been incensed to see my helmet
Destroyed. A hero? Pooh! At heart I was
A petty miser, miserliness being
A dire infection easily picked up
Beneath my father's roof. But, say, how is
My poor Emir?

IVAN

Still lame and in no shape
For you to ride him, sir.

ALBERT

I'll have to buy
The bay, I think: they ask a modest price.

IVAN

Sir, for an empty purse 'tis yet too steep.

ALBERT

What says that beggar Solomon?

IVAN

That he
Can ill afford to loan Your Honour money
Unless you leave a pledge with him.

ALBERT

The devil!
Where would I get one? Did you ask him that?

IVAN

I did.

ALBERT

And what of him?

IVAN

He hemmed and hawed.

ALBERT

You might have told him I'm the son and heir
Of one who is as rich as any Jew.

IVAN

I did.

ALBERT

And what of him?

IVAN

He hawed and hemmed.

ALBERT

Worse luck!

IVAN

He's coming here, he said.

ALBERT

Thank Heaven!
He'll pay me ransom 'fore I let him out.

A knock at the door.

Who's there?

Enter the JEW.

JEW

Your humble servant.

ALBERT

Pray, come in!
I hear, good Solomon, you curséd Jew,
My honoured and esteemed and valued friend,
That you deny me credit?

JEW

Worthy knight,
I should oblige you willingly if I
But had the means!.. Alas! To penury
Am I reduced through having with my purse
Been overgenerous... Now, could you not
Repay in part the sum you owe me?

ALBERT

What?!
You blackguard! Well you know that if I boasted
A fuller pocket, I should never deal
With such as you. But, pray, be not so stubborn,
Sweet Solomon, and count me out a hundred
Gold pieces 'fore I have you searched.

JEW

A hundred?!

I wish I had so many!

ALBERT

Would you, then,
Refuse to help your friend? For shame!

JEW

Good sir,

I swear to you—

ALBERT

Come, come, I'll hear no more!
To ask me for a pledge... 'Tis monstrous, Jew!
What say you to a porker's hide? Nay, truly,
If I had aught to pledge I should have sold it
Long since. You dog! Is not my honest word
Enough for you?

JEW

Your word, knight, while you live,
Has no small weight, I grant you; like as if
It were a magic talisman, the richest
Of Flemish coffers it unlocks for you.
But should you pass it on to me, a poor,
Derided Jew, and die, which God forbid,
Why, then it will be worth no more, methinks,
Than, sir, a key to a discarded casket
Cast by its owner in the sea.

ALBERT

Think you
My father will survive me, Jew?

JEW

Who knows!
'Tis not by us, sir knight, our days are numbered!

A youth may thrive one day, and die the next,
And four bent greybeards on their backs will bear
His body to the grave. The Baron is
In fine, good fettle, and by the grace of God
May live another thirty years or so.

ALBERT

Another thirty years... What fibs you speak!
Why, I'll be fifty then and in no need
Of money, Jew.

JEW

                    You err, sweet sir, for gold
Is a commodity that serves us well,
Whate'er our age, except that to a youth
It is a zealous servant whom he sends
On countless errands, while an old man sees
A friend in it on whom he can depend.

ALBERT

Not so my father. Neither friend nor servant
Is it to him, but an exacting master
Whose cringing slave he is and abject lackey
And faithful watch-dog, one in a kennel kept
And fed on water and on mouldy crusts.
At night he never sleeps but to and fro
Runs barking, while the gold he guards reposes
In coffers... One fine day, I promise you,
'Twill learn to serve me and repose no more.

JEW

Aye, at the Baron's funeral more gold
Than tears will flow. With Heaven's help may you
Secure your fortune 'thout deferment.

ALBERT

                                    Amen!

JEW

But stay...

ALBERT

What now?

JEW

There is a cure, sir knight,
For your complaint.

ALBERT

A cure?

JEW

'Tis only that
I know of someone... He's a Jew and poor,
A druggist.

ALBERT

And a usurer, I take it.
Come, say, is he as full of tricks as you
Or, friend, unlike you, honest?

JEW

Toviy deals
In other things than I: he makes up drops
Miraculous in their effect.

ALBERT

Indeed!

JEW

Add three, Your Honour, to a glass of water,
And 'twill suffice; they have no taste or colour

And cause a man no pain and no discomfort;
Death follows swiftly.

ALBERT

                    Ah, I see! Your man
In poisons traffics.

JEW

              Among other things.

ALBERT

Am I to understand that you would lend me
Instead of gold as many phials of
This venom?

JEW

              Sir, you are disposed to mock me,
While I... I thought that you... In short, I felt
'Twas time, if I may say so, for the Baron
To shuffle off this mortal coil...

ALBERT

                    You dog!
I kill my father! dare you hint a thing
So foul to me!.. Quick, Ivan, seize the rascal!
Know you, you slimy snake, you black-souled Judah,
That with my own two hands I'll hang you from
My gate-post here and now!

JEW

                  Sir knight, have mercy!
I meant no harm.

ALBERT

             Come, Ivan, fetch a rope!

JEW

It was a jest; I have the gold you asked for.

ALBERT

Out of my house, you dog!

Exit the JEW.

Oh, to be so
Debased, and I a knight... 'Tis hard to be
A miser's son... The Jew, you heard him, Ivan,
He dared propose... I'm all a-tremble. Fetch me
A glass of wine... And yet I'm still in need
Of money, curse it!.. You will have to bring
The scoundrel back. Some ink and paper; he
Will want a voucher, sure. Into my presence
You're not to show him, pray remember... Wait!
His gold will smell of poison like the silver
His forbear pocketed... I asked for wine—
Where is it?

IVAN

Sir, I looked: we've not a drop
Left in our stores.

ALBERT

And where's the lot Remon
Sent me from Spain?

IVAN

You had me give the last
Remaining bottle to the blacksmith when
The man was taken ill.

ALBERT

I had forgot.
Some water, then. A plague upon this life!..

I have no choice except to ask the Duke
For his protection; let him force my father
To keep me as befits a man, and not
A mouse that gnaws at breadcrumbs in a cellar.

SCENE II

Vaulted cellar.

BARON

As full of hot impatience as a rake
Before a meeting with an artful temptress
Or artless maid caught in his web of lies,
So did I wait all day for that sweet moment
When I could visit this my secret cache
And faithful chests. O blesséd day! For I
Into my sixth, as yet but half-filled chest,
Can put today this gold that I have hoarded—
The merest handful, true, but treasures grow
Little by little. I do remember reading
Of some great prince who bade his men-at-arms
Each lay of earth a handful at his feet.
This done, there rose a lofty hill before him,
And from its crest the prince could gaze upon
The vale below dotted with snowy tents
And watch the vessels plough the azure sea.
Thus I by bringing here my daily tribute,
However scant, have wrought my own great mount
And from its summit can with pride survey
That over which I rule... All, all I hold
In sway... Like some dark, brooding demon I
Sit on my hidden throne... If so I wish,
Majestic palaces will rise before me,
And lively nymphs, a merry, laughing throng,
Come running to my bloom-filled, scented gardens;
The muses will pay homage to my person
And freedom-loving genius be my slave;
Good, virtue, chastity and sleepless toil
My praises and rewards will humbly seek.
All I need do is call, and on its knees
Into my presence villainy will crawl

And meekly lick my hand and, eager, strive
To search my gaze and read its monarch's will:
All do my bidding; none do I obey...
I am above desires and calm of heart,
Content to know my power's extent and drawing
Joy from my knowledge...

Surveys his treasure.

This that I possess
Seems little enough, and yet it is the solid
Embodiment of human trickery,
Of human cares and tears and prayers and curses.
There is an old doubloon here somewhere... Ah!
This is the one. 'Twas brought me by a widow
Who on her knees, her three young brats beside her,
Outside my window stood and howled and whined
For half the day; it rained and then it stopped
And rained again; pretending to despair,
She never moved; I could have had the hussy
Driven away, but something told me she
Had brought her husband's debt for fear of being
Thrown in a debtor's cell... And this? Thibault
Did bring it me. Where could that knave and idler
Have taken it?.. I doubt it not, he stole it,
Or in the night, upon a forest road
Where lonely horsemen pass—
                              If all the tears,
The blood and sweat the gold here kept did cost
Where by the earth disgorged, a second Flood
Might easily ensue, and in my cellars
I then would drown... Enough! Where is my key?

Prepares to unlock one of the chests.

Each time that I approach this chest of mine
And think to open it, a kind of trembling
And fever seize upon me. 'Tis not fear,
Nay, for I've naught to fear: my sword is with me,
Of gold its honest steel the staunch defender.
'Tis something else, a feeling unexplained
And wondrous strange; the medics do assure us
That there are men who find a sort of relish

In slaughtering their kind. As I insert
The key into the lock, my feelings are
Akin to theirs when in a victim's body
They plunge a knife: 'tis rapture mixed with fear.

Unlocks the chest.

Here's bliss!

Pours in coins.

Into the chest with you; the world
You've roamed enough, man's needs and passions
serving...
Rest here as do the gods up in the heavens,
And may like theirs your slumber be serene!
Today I wish to hold a fête, for so
My fancy bids me do. The chests unlocking,
Beside each one I'll set a lighted candle
And revel in the sight of so much splendour.

*Lights candles and unlocks the chests
one after another.*

What magic brilliance! I'm a prince, I reign
Over a proud and mighty realm; my fame
And happiness and honour rest upon it!
Today I am a prince, I reign... But who
My crown and scepter is to have tomorrow?—
None other than my son, a brainless spendthrift,
Companion to a gang of profligates!..
No sooner have I breathed my last than he
Will here descend, beneath these silent vaults,
A greedy crowd of courtiers, aye, and toadies
Behind him trailing, and my lifeless corpse
Rob of these keys, and, laughing recklessly,
Unlock my chests and let my treasures flow
Into silk pockets full as sieves of holes;
My sacred vessels he will smash, and unctions
For monarchs fit on human offal lavish:
He'll waste and squander all... And I—come, say,
Was't easily these riches I obtained?
Did I throw down my dice as does a gambler

And laughingly rake in the glinting coin?..
None know how many torturous abstentions,
Curbed passions and desires, oppressive thoughts,
Days filled with endless care and sleepless nights
My treasures cost me!.. Yet my son will lightly
Declare his father's heart to have been always
O'ergrown with moss, void of desire, unknowing
Of any stir or pang of conscience... Conscience!—
A sharp-clawed beast that maims the spirit...

                                        Conscience!—
A boring guest who comes, unasked; a rough-tongued,
Impatient creditor; a witch, a ghoul
That snuffs out moonlight and compels the dead
To leave their peaceful graves and walk abroad!..
Nay, first through suffering together scrape
A fortune for yourself, and then we'll see
If carelessly you'll waste what gain you did
At such a price!.. If only I could hide
My cache from greedy eyes!.. If but I could
Rise from my grave, and, perching on a chest,
A vigilant and patient phantom, guard,
As I do now, my treasures from the living!..

SCENE III

In the castle.

ALBERT and the DUKE.

ALBERT

Believe me, sire, I have endured too long
The shame of bitter poverty. Were't not
That I am driven to extremity
I'd not complain.

DUKE

                    Well do I know it, knight.
One like you would not thus accuse his father
Unless provoked. Indeed, few could be so
Depraved as to attempt it... Rest you easy:

I will exhort your father privately,
That none may know of it. He'll be here shortly.
It's been an age since last we met... He was
My grandsire's friend. When I was but a child
It was his wont to seat me on his horse
And place upon my head his helmet that
Was very like a church-bell.

Looks out of the window.

                              Here he comes,
If I mistake not.

ALBERT

Yes, 'tis he.

DUKE

                              My summons
Await in yonder chamber, knight.

Exit ALBERT; enter the BARON.

                              Ah, Baron,
It pleases me to see you in good health.

BARON

I am most happy, sire, to have been able
To muster strength enough to come in answer
To your kind bidding.

DUKE

                              It's been years and years
Since we last met. I hope you still remember
The boy I was.

BARON

                    Indeed, I do. You were
A lively child. The late-lamented Duke

Would say to me: "Filippe,"—it was his custom
Thus to address me—"think you not, Filippe,
That in another twenty years we two
Will seem as fools before this lad?" (He meant
Yourself, Your Grace.)

DUKE

You've kept aloof too long.
We shall, I trust and pray, resume our friendship.

BARON

I'm old and feeble... What would I do at court?
You, being young, are fond of tournaments
And noisy fêtes for which I am unsuited.
Now, if't be Heaven's will that war should come,
Why, then I'll, groaning, climb a horse's back
And find the strength my ancient sword to pull
From out its sheath in your defence.

DUKE

Your zeal
Is known to us; my father held you always
In high esteem as did his own dear father
Whose friend you were. I too did ever think you
To be a brave and loyal knight. Pray, sit.
I know not well: have you a son or daughter?

BARON

A son, Your Grace.

DUKE

Why is't I never see
The lad at court? For one not old and of
His birth and calling, Baron, 'tis but fitting
To be among us.

BARON

Aye, but fond he's not
Of sports and revels, being of a sullen,
Retiring nature. Like a deer he roams
The forests roundabout.

DUKE

'Tis ill that he
In this wise shuns us. But I have great hopes
That we can tame him; he will come to like
Our jousts and balls... I shall expect him here
Without undue delay. And see to't, Baron,
That he has means sufficient for his station.
You look not glad... Perchance, sir, you are weary?

BARON

Nay, that I'm not, Your Grace, but in confusion
Of mind and heart. You force me to confess
What I would rather have revealed to none,
Not e'en yourself. My son, to his and my
Misfortune, is unworthy of your favour
And kind regard. He wastes his youth on wicked
And sinful deeds...

DUKE

If so he does, 'tis likely
That left he is too often to himself.
An over-dose of solitude and leisure
Can be a young man's ruin. Send your son
To us, and he will soon forget the morbid
And sorry habits born of loneliness.

BARON

Forgive me, sire, but disregard I must
Your wish.

DUKE

Why so?

BARON

        Compel me not to answer,
Take pity on my years.

DUKE

        No, Baron, I
Demand to hear why you refuse to heed
The little that I ask of you.

BARON

        'Tis only
That I am wroth with him.

DUKE

        What has he done?

BARON

An evil thing.

DUKE

        Enlighten me, I beg.

BARON

Allow me to refrain.

DUKE

        'Tis odd! You seem
Ashamed to voice your thoughts...

BARON

        Aye, that I am.

DUKE

Still, I insist: what has he done?

BARON

He tried...
To kill me, sire.

DUKE

What?! He will pay for this
Black piece of villainy!

BARON

I'll not essay
To give you proof of it, well as I know
How much he craves my death, and well as I
Know that he went so far as to attempt...
To ... to...

DUKE

Speak out.

BARON

To rob me, sire.

ALBERT rushes in.

ALBERT

You lie!

DUKE

to ALBERT

How dared you?!—

BARON

You?! Thus to insult your father!
What flagrant insolence! To say I lie
Before the Duke, our lord and suzerain!
Am I no more a knight?..

ALBERT

You are a liar!

BARON

And he not stricken down by thunder! Come,
Pick up my glove! The sword will be our judge!

Flings down his glove;
ALBERT hastens to pick it up.

ALBERT

My father's gift, his first. I thank you, Baron.

DUKE

Has this I witnessed truly come to pass?
A son takes up his agéd father's challenge!
O, what a fearsome age is this in which
I donned the ducal chain!.. Speak not, you

madman!

And you, young tiger, silence! I will have
No more of this, you hear? The glove!

Takes the glove away from Albert.

ALBERT

(aside)

A pity!

DUKE

He fairly dug his claws in it, the villain!
Go! Leave my chamber. I will not support
Your presence longer. Come when you are called
And not before.

Exit ALBERT.

And you, old man, for shame!
A wretched business this!..

BARON

     Forgive me, sire.
'Tis faint I feel... My legs give under me...
I cannot breathe... Air!.. Give me air!..

         My keys!..
My keys! Where are they!..

DUKE

      He is dead... O God!
What evil times! What black and evil hearts!

1830

Mozart and Salieri

A room.

SALIERI

They say: there is no justice here on earth.
But there is none—hereafter. To my mind
This truth is elementary as a scale.
I was born with a great love of music;
When I was still a child and heard the organ
Resounding through the ancient church at home
I listened—lost in listening—and wept
Involuntary tears of pure delight.
Full early I renounced all idle pleasures
And to all sciences but that of music
I made myself a stranger; with dour pride
I turned my back on them to give myself
Wholly to music. Hard is the first step
And lonely the beginning of the road.
I weathered the first storms. And as a footstool
To art I set perfection in my craft.
And I became a craftsman: taught my fingers
A disciplined, dry fluency, my ear
Exact discrimination. Music I
Dissected like a corpse. Proved its harmonies
Like higher mathematics.
And only then, well-versed in theory,
Did I permit myself the luxury
Of composition. I began
To work; but secretly, but in retirement,
Not daring to so much as think of fame.

And times there were when I would sit alone
Two, three days, with no thought of food or sleep,
In tears, in ecstasies of inspiration,
Then burn my work and watch indifferently
How all my thoughts, the sounds born of my labour,
Would flare and vanish in a puff of smoke.
But what of that? Why—when the mighty Glück
Appeared to introduce us to new secrets
(Such fathomless, such captivating secrets)
Did I not set at naught all I had learnt,
All I had loved, all I had so believed in?
Did I not follow him with eager tread,
As uncomplaining as an erring traveller
Chance-met with one who better knows the road?
By diligence and unremitting effort,
I rose through the infinity of art,
Attaining high degree. Fame looked my way
And smiled; my harmonies began to find
An echo, a response in people's hearts.
And I was happy: I took quiet pleasure
In work, success and fame; rejoicing also
To see the work of friends crowned by success,
My colleagues in the service of high art.
No! Never did I know the sting of envy.
Oh, never! Neither when Piccini charmed
The ear and favour of barbaric Paris,
Nor yet when I first heard the cadences
Of my great teacher's *Iphigenia.*
Who dares to say that proud Salieri ever
Was subject to the most despised of vices,
Impotent envy, writhing, weak, down-trodden,
A dust-choked serpent on the public highway?
Why—no one! But today—myself I say it—
Today I envy I am consumed by deep,
Tormenting envy. Oh, celestial Justice!
Where are you now when the most sacred gift,
Immortal genius, is not sent to bless
The ardent lover, the devout ascetic,
A fit reward for toil and prayerful vigil,
But haloes a gregarious trifler's head,
A carefree lunatic's—Oh, Mozart, Mozart!

Enter MOZART.

MOZART

Aha! You saw me! And I meant to treat you
To a surprise, something to make you laugh.

SALIERI

You here!—When did you come?

MOZART

Just now. I have
Something to show you and was on my way here
When, as I passed the inn, a fiddler's scraping
Assailed my ears... Oh no, my friend, Salieri!
You never in your life heard anything
So comical... A tavern fiddler struggling,
To execute *voi che sapete*. Marvellous!
I simply had to bring the man along
To treat you to a sample of his art.
Come in!

Enter an old blind man with a fiddle.

Now, be so good, something from Mozart.

The old man plays an aria from
DON JUAN. *Mozart is overcome with laughter.*

SALIERI

And you can laugh at that?

MOZART

My dear Salieri,
But how can you help laughing?

SALIERI

Easily.
It does not make me laugh when a poor painter

Attempts to copy Raphael's Madonna.
It does not make me laugh when a vile rhymster
Dishonours Dante by bad imitation.
Be gone, old man.

MOZART

       One moment, here, take this
And drink my health, good fellow.

Exit the old man.

          You, Salieri,
Are out of sorts today. I'll come to see you
Some other time.

SALIERI

What did you have to show me?

MOZART

Oh—nothing much, a trifle. The other night
I could not get to sleep—my old insomnia—
And two or three ideas came to my mind.
Today I wrote them down. I would have liked you
To give me your opinion of them, but
You are not in the mood.

SALIERI

     Ah Mozart, Mozart!
Not in the mood to hear you play?! Sit down;
I'm listening.

MOZART

(at the fortepiano)

     Imagine ... whom you would...
Me, if you like—but just a little younger;
In love—but not too deeply, just a fancy;
A Beauty, or a friend—say, you—beside me,

In high spirits... Then, suddenly: a darkness,
A vision of the grave, or some such thing...
Well, better listen.

Plays.

SALIERI

You brought that to me
And on the way could stop outside a tavern
To hear that old blind fiddler scrape!.. Good God!
You, Mozart, are not worthy of yourself.

MOZART

You like it then?

SALIERI

But what profundity!
What boldness and what harmony of form!
You, Mozart, are a god and do not know it;
But I know, I.

MOZART

Bah! Do you think so?
But now my godship badly wants its dinner.

SALIERI

I have a notion: Let us dine together.
The Golden Lion's a decent inn.

MOZART

With pleasure;
I should enjoy that. But first I must go home
And tell my wife not to expect me back
To dine today.

Exit.

SALIERI

I shall expect you; fail not.
No! I can no more resist the fate
To which I am appointed; it is my task
To stop him. If I do not, all of us,
The priests, the celebrants of music, perish.
Not I alone with my small part of fame...
What is the use if Mozart is to live
And to attain new heights, undreamed of summits?
Will he by this raise music? No, he will not.
It will fall back again with his extinction.
For he will leave no heir to lead us on.
What use is he? Like some bright Cherub
He came down with a sheaf of songs divine
But to wake wingless longings in the hearts
Of us poor sons of dust—then fly away!
Fly, fly then Mozart! Fly! As soon as may be.

Here's poison, the last gift of my Izora.
I've kept it by me now for eighteen years—
How often in this span has life inflicted
Wounds unendurable; how often have I sat
At board with an all-unsuspecting foe,
Yet never hearkened to the insistent whisper
Of sharp temptation, though I am no coward,
Though deeply sensitive to injury,
Though I hold life but cheap. Still I delayed.
And when the death-wish came to torture me,
Why, what is death? I thought: it may be life
Will shower me yet with unexpected gifts;
It may be ecstasy will come again,
And rapture, and a night of inspiration;
It may be some new Haydn will compose
Some work of greatness that will give me pleasure...
Or, when I feasted with some odious guest,
Perhaps I thought to meet an enemy
More deadly; some more deadly injury, perhaps,
Might strike me from the contumelious heights—
Then, then Izora's gift would prove most useful.
And I was right! And now at last I've found
My enemy, and a new Haydn has
Awoken me to ecstasy divine!

Now—it is time! Oh, cherished gift of love,
Today you pass into the cup of friendship.

SCENE II

> *Private room at the inn; a fortepiano.*
> *MOZART and SALIERI at table.*

SALIERI

You're dull today and gloomy! Why?

MOZART

I? No!

SALIERI

Has something happened, Mozart, to upset you?
The dinner's good, the wine is of the best,
But you sit silent, frowning...

MOZART

I confess
It is my Requiem perturbs me.

SALIERI

Ah!
You are composing a Requiem! Since when?

MOZART

A long time now—three weeks. But was rather
strange...
Did not I tell you?

SALIERI

No.

MOZART

Then listen.
Three weeks ago today I came home late
And I was told: a visitor had called
To see me. He did not state his business.
All night I wondered: who could it have been?
What did he want of me? And the next day
He called again. Again I was from home.
The third day I was playing on the floor
With my small son. Somebody called me out.
I came. A man, all dressed in mourning black,
Gave me a civil bow, requested me
To write a Requiem, and left. I set
To work at once... But since that time the man
In black has never come to claim his order...
And, in a way, I'm glad. I should be sorry
To see my work pass on. The Requiem,
However, is quite ready. But I...

SALIERI

But you?

MOZART

I feel ashamed now to admit it...

SALIERI

What?

MOZART

By night and day my man in black still haunts
Me. Like a shadow he trails after me
Wherever I direct my steps. Ev'n now
It seems to me he makes a third with us
At table.

SALIERI

Oh, come! A childish fancy, nothing more!
Such fears are groundless. Shake them off! My friend

Beaumarchais used to say: "Brother Salieri,
When black thoughts trouble you, the golden cure
Is to uncork a bottle of champagne
Or read *Le Mariage de Figaro*."

MOZART

Of course! Beaumarchais was a friend of yours;
It was for him that you composed *Tarare*,
A pleasant opera. There is one tune there...
I always hum it when I'm feeling happy...
La la la la... Ah, is it true, Salieri,
That Beaumarchais once poisoned somebody?

SALIERI

I do not think so: he was too amusing
For such grim business.

MOZART

            He was a genius,
Like you and me. And villainy and genius
Are incompatibles. Am I not right?

SALIERI

You think so?

    Shakes the poison into MOZART's glass.

    But you do not drink.

MOZART

                  Your health,
My friend, and long live the true tie
Which binds together Mozart and Salieri,
Two sons of harmony, of music.

    Drinks.

SALIERI

Wait!
Wait, wait!.. Ah, you have drunk it!.. Without me?

MOZART

Casts his napkin on the table.

Enough, I want no more.

Goes to the fortepiano.

And now, Salieri,
My Requiem.

Plays.

You're weeping?

SALIERI

I have never
Wept tears like these before, both sweet and bitter,
As though a dreadful weight of obligation
Had fallen from me, or the healing knife
Had mercifully severed a spoilt limb!
Good Mozart, do not heed these tears. Go on,
Make haste to satiate my soul with sounds...

MOZART

If only everyone so felt the power
Of harmony! But no: for then, most likely,
The world would stop: no one would take the trouble
To care for the base needs of common life;
All would devote themselves to art in freedom,
How few we are: the carefree and elect
Who can afford to scorn utility
And serve as zealots of the one God—Beauty.
Is that not so? But I'm not well today.
A heaviness is on me; I will go and sleep.
Good-bye then!

SALIERI

Fare you well.

Alone.

                              Your sleep will last
A long while, Mozart! Could it be he's right
And I no genius? Villainy and genius
Are incompatibles. It cannot be.
And Buonarotti? Was he calumniated
By foolish rumour? Did the man who built
The Vatican in fact commit no murder?

1830

The Stone Guest

LEPORELLO: O statua gentilissima
Del gran' Commendatore!..
...Ah, Padrone!

DON GIOVANNI

SCENE I

DON JUAN and LEPORELLO.

DON JUAN

Here we'll await the night. Aha, at last
We've reached Madrid. Here are the gates—and soon
I shall be stealing down familiar streets
Moustachios muffled in my cloak, hat tilted
To hide my brows. How's that? Will no one know me?

LEPORELLO

Of course, it's hard to recognise Don Juan!
There are so many like him!

DON JUAN

You'll never say so?
Why, who's to know me?

LEPORELLO

Sir, the first night watchman,
Or Gypsy slut, or drunken street musician,
Or your own sort, some thrusting caballero,
A sword tucked in his armpit, closely cloaked.

DON JUAN

So be it, then! It matters not. I'd rather
Not meet the King, though. Still—what if I do?
There's not a soul I fear in all Madrid.

LEPORELLO

But when it reaches the King's ears tomorrow:
Don Juan to his capital unsummoned
From exile has returned—what then, I ask you?
What will he do to you?

DON JUAN

     Why—send me back.
I'm very sure he'll not chop off my head.
I stand not, after all, accused of crimes
Against the state. He banished me in love
So that the relatives of him I slew
Might not molest me.

LEPORELLO

     Well, there you are then,
Why not stay put—and thank him?

DON JUAN

        Very near
I came to dying of boredom there. The people!
The land itself! The sky?.. A pall of smoke.
The women? Why, my foolish Leporello,
I'd not exchange—d'you hear me, stupid fellow?—
The lowest of our Andalusian peasants
For their most dazzling beauties—truly not.
They pleased me to begin with, I admit it,
Because their eyes were blue, their skins were white,
They—modest, with the chasm of novelty!
But soon, the Lord be praised, I realised—
I saw quite clearly there was nothing to them—
No life—a waste of time—like waxen dolls;
But ours now!.. Hey, look there, this place—
            it seems
Familiar; do you know it?

LEPORELLO

Of course I know it.
I've reason to remember St. Anthony's.
You left me in that grove to hold the horses,
A tiresome task, believe me! You, good master,
Spent your time here more pleasantly than I did,
I do assure you.

DON JUAN

(thoughtfully)

My poor, sad Ineza!
She is no more! How much I loved her once!

LEPORELLO

Ineza!—that black-eyed wench! I mind me
It took three months to win her, and the devil
I think it was who helped you at the last.

DON JUAN

It was July ... at night. A strange enchantment
I found in her sad eyes, in her numb lips.
How strange. You, I remember, Leporello,
Did not admire her. And indeed she was not
A real beauty. It was just the eyes,
The eyes and then—the way she looked... A look
Such as I have not met in any other.
Her voice was quiet and weak—like a sick woman's.
Her husband was a ruthless brute, a villain,
I found that out too late—my poor Ineza!..

LEPORELLO

What of it, others followed.

DON JUAN

That's true, too.

LEPORELLO

And if we live, there will be others yet.

DON JUAN

And that.

LEPORELLO

      And now which one are we to visit
In dark Madrid this evening?

DON JUAN

        Laura, of course!
I shall go straight to greet her.

LEPORELLO

         Come, that's better!

DON JUAN

In at the door—and if some other guest
Sits in my place—he'll go out by the window!

LEPORELLO

As is but fitting. Come now, we are merry,
Dead ladies do not hold our thoughts for long.
Who comes to meet us?

      Enter a MONK.

THE MONK

        She is on her way here,
But who is this? People of Doña Anna's?

LEPORELLO

No, our own masters we, and walk here for
Our pleasure.

DON JUAN

But who is it you wait for?

THE MONK

I wait for Doña Anna, who will come
Here to her husband's graveside.

DON JUAN

                          Doña Anna
De Solva! What! The wife of the Commander
Killed by... I don't remember whom?

THE MONK

                          The godless,
Unscrupulous and most depraved Don Juan.

LEPORELLO

Oho! Indeed! Don Juan's reputation
Has even found a way to peaceful cloisters
And hermits sing his praises in their cells.

THE MONK

Perhaps you know him?

LEPORELLO

                          Know him? Not at all.
Where is he now, though?

THE MONK

                          He is far away,
Exiled to distant lands.

LEPORELLO.

                          And a good riddance,
The further off, the better. I would clap
A sack over such rakes and drown them all.

DON JUAN

What, what's that you say?

LEPORELLO

Be quiet: a ruse, Sir...

DON JUAN

So it was here they buried the Commander?

THE MONK

Here; and his wife raised him a monument
And comes to visit it each day to pray
For his departed spirit and to weep
Upon the grave.

DON JUAN

What an unusual widow!
And not bad-looking?

THE MONK

Woman's beauty should
Not move us hermits. But to lie is sin;
Even a saint of God could not deny
That she is wonderfully beautiful.

DON JUAN

The dead man had good reason to be jealous.
He kept his Doña Anna locked away.
Not one of us has even set eyes upon her.
I'd like to have a word with her myself.

THE MONK

Ah no, it is a rule of Doña Anna's
Not to converse with men.

DON JUAN

But you, my father?

THE MONK

With me it's quite another thing; my cloth...
But here she comes.

Enter DOÑA ANNA.

DOÑA ANNA

Good Father, unlock the gates.

THE MONK

At once, Señora; I was waiting for you.

DOÑA ANNA follows the MONK out.

LEPORELLO

Well, how was she?

DON JUAN

Not to be seen at all
Behind the blackness of those widow's weeds.
I only caught a glimpse of a slim heel.

LEPORELLO

Enough for you. Your own imagination
Will fill in other details quick as thought;
It can complete a picture like a painter
And 'tis all one to it where to begin—
With brows, or ankles.

DON JUAN

Listen, Leporello,
I shall make her acquaintance.

LEPORELLO

Oh, you will!
A fine idea! First you dispatch the husband
And then you pry upon the widow's tears.
No shame at all!

DON JUAN

Look, though, the night has fallen!
Before the moonrise overtakes us here,
And turns the darkness into shining dusk
We must be in Madrid.

Exit.

LEPORELLO

A Spanish grandee,
And like a common thief he waits for nightfall
And fears the moonrise. What a life—oh Lord!
How long must I be bothering my head
With all his freakish starts? This last's the limit!

SCENE II

A room. Supper at LAURA's.

FIRST GUEST

I'll take my oath, dear Laura, that you never
Before played so divinely as this evening.
How perfectly you understood your part.

SECOND

A fine interpretation! And such power!

THIRD

Such art!

LAURA

Why yes, it was as though for me
Today there could be no false word or gesture.
I yielded freely to my inspiration.
The words poured forth, not slavishly by rote,
But from the heart—my own words.

FIRST

Yes, indeed.
And even now your eyes are shining bright,
Your cheeks are glowing, inspiration still
Flames high within you. Laura, do not let it
Grow cold all unadmired; sing to us, Laura,
Sing something new.

LAURA

Then hand me my guitar.

Sings.

ALL

O *brava! brava!* Wonderful! Superb!

FIRST

We thank you, sorceress. You weave your charms
About our hearts. Of all life's pleasures
Music yields pride of place to love alone,
And even love's—a melody ... just look
Even Carlos here is moved, your dourest guest.

SECOND

What numbers! How they play upon the heartstrings!
Whose are the words, dear Laura, pray?

LAURA

Don Juan's.

DON CARLOS

What's that? Don Juan!

LAURA

Yes—a trifle written
By my true friend, my reckless, hare-brained lover.

DON CARLOS

Your damnable Don Juan's a godless rake-hell,
And you—you are a fool!

LAURA

Have you gone mad?
I'll call my servants now to slit your gullet
Though you were twenty times grandee of Spain.

DON CARLOS

Rises.

Go, call them then.

FIRST

Laura, that's enough,
Don Carlos, don't be angry. She forgot...

LAURA

What? That Don Juan killed his brother
In fair fight, in a duel? True: the more's
The pity it was not him.

DON CARLOS

I was a fool
To lose my temper.

LAURA

Ha! So you admit it.
Let's make it up, then—fool!

DON CARLOS

                    I'm sorry, Laura,
Forgive me. But you know I cannot hear
That name unmoved...

LAURA

                    But can I help it if
That name is always on my lips, Don Carlos?

A GUEST

Come now, to prove you are no longer angry,
Dear Laura, sing again.

LAURA

                    I will—in farewell.
The night has fallen. What shall I sing? Aha!
I have it—listen!

Sings.

ALL

Charming, quite superb!

LAURA

Good-bye then, gentlemen!

GUESTS

                    Good-bye, dear Laura.

Exeunt. LAURA halts DON CARLOS.

LAURA

You, fire-eater, will stay with me.
I like you; you remind me of Don Juan,
The way you swore at me and ground your teeth
So fiercely.

DON CARLOS

Fortunate man! You loved him?

LAURA makes a gesture of assent.

You loved him very much?

LAURA

Yes, very much.

DON CARLOS

And do you love him still?

LAURA

What, now, this minute?
No, I do not. I can't love two at once.
Now it is you I love.

DON CARLOS

Then tell me, Laura,
How old are you?

LAURA

I am eighteen years old.

DON CARLOS

That's very young ... and you will still be young
For five years more, or six. And men will flock
For six years more to bring you gifts and cozen
Your favour with caresses and soft words
And sooth your ear with midnight serenades,
And even slaughter one another for you
At night upon the crossroads. But—when that time
Is past, and when your eyes grow cavernous
And over them the lids are dark and puckered,
When the first few grey hairs gleam in your braids,

And they begin to call you an old woman,
What then—what say you?

LAURA

              Then? What then? Why
Should I think of that? Why do you talk of it?
Or do your thoughts always run on that way?
Come here, open the window. How quiet the sky is!
The warm air hangs so still—and the night smells
Of lemon and of bay, the moon shines bright
Against the deepening blueness of the dark—
And the night-watch calls his long-drawn: *sereno!..*
And far away—far to the North—in Paris,
It may be that the sky is thick with clouds,
A chilly drizzle falls and the wind blows—
But what is that to us? Come now, Don Carlos,
I order you to smile, now, I command it.
That's it!

DON CARLOS

Bewitching demon!

A sound of knocking.

DON JUAN

           Hey there! Laura!

LAURA

Who's there? Whose voice is that?

DON JUAN

             Come, open up...

LAURA

It could not!.. Oh my God!..

Unlocks the door. Enter DON JUAN.

DON JUAN

Good evening...

LAURA

Juan!..

LAURA flings herself on his neck.

DON CARLOS

How's this! Don Juan!..

DON JUAN

Laura, darling heart!

Kisses her.

Who is this here with you, my Laura?

DON CARLOS

Don Carlos!

DON JUAN

What an unexpected pleasure!
Tomorrow I'll be happy to oblige you...

DON CARLOS

No! Now—at once!

LAURA

Don Carlos, that will do!
You are not in the street—you're in my home—
Be good enough to leave us.

DON CARLOS

(ignoring her)

I am waiting.
Come, man, you have a sword.

DON JUAN

Since you are so
Impatient—as you will.

They fight.

LAURA

Oy! Oy! Oh, Juan!..

Casts herself on the bed.

DON CARLOS falls.

DON JUAN

Get up! It's over, Laura.

LAURA

What has happened?
You've killed him! Wonderful! In my apartment!
Now what am I to do, you rake-hell devil?
Where can I dump the body?

DON JUAN

Wait—perhaps
He's still alive.

LAURA

(examining the corpse)

Alive indeed! Look, damn you,
Straight to the heart—you wouldn't miss, not you!
A neat, three-cornered wound—no blood at all,
And he's not breathing—well?

DON JUAN

What could I do?
He brought it on himself.

LAURA

Ah, Juan, Juan,
It's very tiresome. Always up to mischief—
And always not your fault... Where did you come from?
Have you been back long?

DON JUAN

I have just arrived.
And secretly at that—without a pardon...

LAURA

And straight away you thought about your Laura!
That was well done, I must admit. But no,
I don't believe you! You just happened to be
Passing and saw my house.

DON JUAN

Oh no, my Laura,
Ask Leporello. I am putting up
Outside the town in an accursed venta.
I braved Madrid for Laura.

Kisses her.

LAURA

My beloved!
But stop!.. before the dead!.. Where can we put him?

DON JUAN

Why, leave him there—before the dawn I'll take him
Beneath my cloak and carry him away
And lay him on the crossroads.

LAURA

                              Good, but take
Good care that no one recognises you.
How well it was you came no earlier than
You did! Some friends of yours were with me here.
We had just finished supper, and they but gone
A moment since. What if you should have met them?

DON JUAN

Come, tell me, Laura, have you loved him long?

LAURA

Why, who? You must be raving.

DON JUAN

                              Then confess.
Tell me how many times you have betrayed me
While I have been away.

LAURA

                    And you, you scamp?

DON JUAN

Tell me ... but no, we'll have just this out—but—after!

SCENE III

The Commander's Statue.

DON JUAN

So—all is for the best: since I was careless
Enough to kill Don Carlos I've been hiding
Dressed as a humble hermit here, where daily
I see my charming widow and, it seems,
Myself go not unnoticed. Up till now

We've kept each other at a civil distance;
Today I'll speak with her: the time is ripe.
How to begin? "I make so bold..." or, no!
"Señora..." bah! I had best not rehearse
But say the first thing that comes to my mind,
Even as I improvise my songs of love...
The poor Commander is quite dull without her.
What an Olympian they've made of him!
What shoulders! What a Hercules he looks!
Whereas the dead man was but short and weedy...
Here, had he stood on tiptoe, he could not
Have touched his own nose with one fingertip.
And when we met behind th' Escurial,
Pinpointed on my sword he ceased to struggle
Light as a grasshopper—yet he was
Both proud and brave—a man of sternest spirit...
Ah! Here she comes.

Enter DOÑA ANNA.

DOÑA ANNA

                    Again he's here! Good father,
I have disturbed you at your meditations—
Forgive me.

DON JUAN

                    It is I should ask forgiveness
Of you, Señora. Do not I inhibit
The free expression of your pious sorrow?

DOÑA ANNA

No, father, for my sorrow is within me,
And in your presence my poor prayers may rise
In all humility to heaven—pray join
Your voice with mine in common supplication.

DON JUAN

Me, me to pray with you! Ah, Doña Anna!
I am not worthy of so great an honour,

I would not dare to move these sinful lips
In repetition of your holy prayers,
And only from the distance, reverently,
I watch you as you quietly kneel down
And lay your black head on the pallid marble
Your hair all flowing loose—some angel, then,
You seem, come secretly to this poor grave,
But in my troubled heart no prayer wells up
At such a moment. Silent, marvelling,
I stand and think—how happy he whose marble,
Cold tomb is warmed by her live breath divine
And watered by her tender, loving tears...

DOÑA ANNA

What a—strange way you speak!

DON JUAN

How so, Señora?

DOÑA ANNA

I... You forget.

DON JUAN

What? That I am an humble,
Unworthy hermit? That my sinful voice
Should not ring out so loudly in this place?

DOÑA ANNA

It seemed to me ... I did not understand.

DON JUAN

Alas, I see; you know it all now, all!

DOÑA ANNA

What do I know?

DON JUAN

Why, that I am no monk—
Forgive me! At your feet I beg forgiveness...

DOÑA ANNA

Ah God! Get up, get up... Who are you, then?

DON JUAN

Unhappy victim of a hopeless passion.

DOÑA ANNA

Oh Heaven! Even here, beside this grave!
Leave me at once.

DON JUAN

One moment, Doña Anna.
One moment!

DOÑA ANNA

What if someone should come!

DON JUAN

The grid is locked. Grant me one moment!

DOÑA ANNA

Well? What? What would you ask of me?

DON JUAN

My death!
If only I could die now at your feet
Then my poor body might be buried here,
Not near that one you love, not here, not even
Close by, but somewhere further from the tomb.
There—by the doors—beneath the very threshold,

That you might touch the stone slab with your feet
Or brush it lightly with your garment's hem,
When you come here to visit this proud grave
And bow your trembling curls, and weep.

DOÑA ANNA

                                                    I think
You are demented.

DON JUAN

                        Is it then a sign
Of madness, Doña Anna, to crave death?
I should be mad indeed had I desired
To live, for then I must have lived in hope
That my most tender love might touch your heart;
Had I been a madman, I'd have spent
Whole nights beneath your balcony, and kept
You from your sleep with serenades and music;
I would not have disguised myself, but rather
Have sought t'intrude myself upon your notice;
If I had been a madman, I would not
Have suffered thus in silence.

DOÑA ANNA

                              Would you say
That this was suffering in silence?

DON JUAN

                                Chance, pure chance
Led me to break in—were it not for that
You never would have known of my sad secret.

DOÑA ANNA

And have you loved me long?

DON JUAN

                              Long, or not long,
I do not know myself; I only know

That only since then have I felt the value
Of this ephemeral life, only since then
Found out what the word "happiness" might mean.

DOÑA ANNA

Leave me at once—you are a dangerous man.

DON JUAN

I—dangerous! How?

DOÑA ANNA

I fear to listen to you.

DON JUAN

I say no more; but order not away
One whose whole joy in life is to behold you.
I nourish no brash, overweening hopes,
I ask for nothing, only I must continue
To see you, if indeed I am condemned
To go on living.

DOÑA ANNA

Go—this is no place
For speeches such as these, for such wild ravings.
Tomorrow you may come to me. But swear
To hold me in no less respect and honour.
I shall receive you—later—in the evening—
I have seen no one since the day when I
Was widowed...

DON JUAN

Angel, Doña Anna!
God give you comfort, even as you today
Have comforted this poor, unhappy sufferer.

DOÑA ANNA

But leave me now alone.

DON JUAN

One moment more.

DOÑA ANNA

Indeed, I see that I shall have to leave.
Moreover, I have lost the mind for prayer.
You have distracted me with worldly speeches.
It's long, aye, very long since I heard such.
Tomorrow you may come...

DON JUAN

I cannot yet believe
In my good fortune, dare not yet rejoice.
I shall see you tomorrow! And not here,
Not secretly!

DOÑA ANNA

Tomorrow, yes, tomorrow.
What is your name?

DON JUAN

Diego de Calvado.

DOÑA ANNA

Good-bye then, Don Diego.

Exit.

DON JUAN

Leporello!

Enter LEPORELLO.

LEPORELLO

What can I do for you?

DON JUAN

O Leporello!
I'm happy! Late—tomorrow evening...
Good fellow, make you ready ... tomorrow...
I'm happy as a child!

LEPORELLO

Can you have spoken
To Doña Anna? Perhaps she cast you
A kindly word or two, or could it be
You've given her your blessing, holy father?

DON JUAN

No, Leporello, no! A rendezvous,
I have a rendezvous!

LEPORELLO

Well, I'll be...
O widows, you are all alike!

DON JUAN

I'm happy
I could embrace the whole wide world and sing.

LEPORELLO

But what will the Commander have to say?

DON JUAN

You think he might be jealous? Surely not,
He is a reasonable man and has
Had time to cool his hot blood underground.

LEPORELLO

No; just look at his statue.

DON JUAN

Well, what of it?

LEPORELLO

It seems to me his eyes are fixed on you
In anger...

DON JUAN

Really? Then, good Leporello,
Go beg the honour of his company
At my—oh no!—at Doña Anna's house.

LEPORELLO

Invite a statue! Why!

DON JUAN

Certainly not
To pass the time in idle conversation!
Step forward, bid the statue come stand sentry
At Doña Anna's door late in the evening,
Tomorrow night.

LEPORELLO

You have strange tastes in jest.
Think who he is!

DON JUAN

Step forward!

LEPORELLO

But...

DON JUAN

Go on!

LEPORELLO

Most glorious and honourable of statues!
My master here, Don Juan, humbly begs
You to attend... I swear I cannot say it.
I am afraid.

DON JUAN

Poltroon! Take care!

LEPORELLO

All right then.
My master here, Don Juan, does invite you
Tomorrow late to stand before the doors
Of your good lady's home...

The statue nods its head in consent.

Ay!

DON JUAN

What now?

LEPORELLO

Ay, ay,
Ay, ay!.. I'm dying!

DON JUAN

What's the matter with you?

LEPORELLO

(nodding his head)

The statue... Ay!..

DON JUAN

You're bowing!

LEPORELLO

No, not I,
It bowed its head!

DON JUAN

What drivel you do talk!

LEPORELLO

Go see yourself.

DON JUAN

Then watch me, worthless lout.

(To the statue)

Commander, I invite you to your widow's
Home, where I too shall be—tomorrow night.
To mount guard at her doors. What? Will you come?

The statue nods again.

Oh God!

LEPORELLO

I told you...

DON JUAN

Let's go out of here.

SCENE IV

DOÑA ANNA's room.
DON JUAN and DOÑA ANNA.

DOÑA ANNA

I have received you, Don Diego, but I fear
That my sad conversation will but bore you.

A grieving widow I, who cannot but remember
Her loss each moment. And my smiles are mingled
And mixed with tears like April. Tell me why
Do you say nothing?

DON JUAN

                Indeed, my joy's too deep
For words ... to know myself alone at last
With beauteous Doña Anna, here—not there,
Not by the graveside of the happy dead,
To see you so, and not upon your knees
Before a marble husband.

DOÑA ANNA

             Don Diego,
So you are jealous—can it be my husband
Torments you even from the grave?

DON JUAN

                    I have
No right. You chose him.

DOÑA ANNA

                No, it was my mother
Who bade me give my hand to Don Alvar,
For we were poor, and Don Alvar was rich.

DON JUAN

Fortunate man! He brought his empty treasures
And laid them at a Goddess' feet, for which
He was rewarded by divine delight! If only
I had but met you sooner—with what joy
I would have offered rank and fortune—all,
For but one sweet look of encouragement!
A slave, I would have held your least wish sacred
And studied all your whims to satisfy them
Before you knew yourself what you were lacking,
To make your life uninterrupted magic...
Alas for me that this was not to be.

DOÑA ANNA

Diego, say no more: it is a sin
For me to listen, for I may not love you.
A widow should keep faith beyond the grave.
If you but knew—my husband loved me so!
Ah, Don Alvar would never, I am certain,
Have entertained some poor, enamoured lady,
Had he been widowed—he would have been true
To nuptial ties.

DON JUAN

                    Do not torment my heart
By constantly recalling, Doña Anna,
Your husband's name. Spare me this punishment.
Though I may well deserve it.

DOÑA ANNA

                         Why? Deserve it?
You are not bound like me by sacred ties
To anyone—is it not so? And by
Your love you injure neither me, not heaven.

DON JUAN

Not injure you! Oh God!

DOÑA ANNA

                         Have you then done me
Some injury? Confess, what was it?

DON JUAN

                                        No,
No, never.

DOÑA ANNA

           But, Diego, what's the matter?
You've wronged me in some way? In what? Pray tell me.

DON JUAN

Not for the world.

DOÑA ANNA

Diego, this is strange.
I beg you, I command you.

DON JUAN

No, oh no.

DOÑA ANNA

So this is how you would obey my will!
What was it you were telling me just now?
How gladly you'd have served me as a slave?
I shall be angry, Don Diego. Answer
What is your guilt before me? Say!

DON JUAN

I dare not,
I would not have you hate me—and you will.

DOÑA ANNA

No, no. Already you have my forgiveness,
But I will know...

DON JUAN

Ah, do not wish to know
So horrible, so murderous a secret.

DOÑA ANNA

So horrible! But you say so on purpose
To torture me with curiosity—what is it?
How could you injure me? I did not know you.
And as for enemies—I have none now
Nor ever have had. With the sole exception
Of him who slew my husband.

DON JUAN

(to himself)

Here it comes!
Now tell me: the unfortunate Don Juan—
Do you know him?

DOÑA ANNA

Why no, I've never set eyes
Upon the man.

DON JUAN

But in your heart do you
Nurse enmity towards him?

DOÑA ANNA

As a duty!
Obliged by honour. But you try to turn
The conversation. Don Diego, Sir—
Now, I demand...

DON JUAN

What would you do if you
Should meet Don Juan?

DOÑA ANNA

I'd plunge my dagger
Into the villain's heart.

DON JUAN

Then, Doña Anna,
Where is your knife? My heart is here.

DOÑA ANNA

Diego!
Why?

DON JUAN

I am not Diego, I am Juan.

DOÑA ANNA

Oh Heavens! No, it cannot be, I will not
Believe...

DON JUAN

I am Don Juan.

DOÑA ANNA

No.

DON JUAN

I killed
Your husband: I have no regrets for what I did
Nor is there in my soul the least remorse.

DOÑA ANNA

Must I believe mine ears? No, no, it cannot be.

DON JUAN

I am Don Juan, and I love you.

DOÑA ANNA

(falling)

Ah!
Where am I?.. Where am I? I'm faint...

DON JUAN

What's wrong with her? What is it, Doña Anna?
Good God!

Get up, get up, wake up, come to Diego,
Your slave is at your feet.

DOÑA ANNA

Leave me alone.

(Faintly)

Ah, you're my enemy, and you have robbed me
Of all, that in this life...

DON JUAN

My dearest love!
I will redeem this blow with all I have.
See, at your feet I wait your last command.
Speak—and I die; speak—and I shall live on
For you alone...

DOÑA ANNA

So this is that Don Juan...

DON JUAN

Who was described to you—am I not right?—
As an inhuman villain, Doña Anna!
It may be that repute in part speaks sooth,
There is, perhaps, much evil weighing on
My weary conscience. For instance, it is true
That I was long apprenticed to debauch
But—so it seems to me—since I first saw you
I've been as one regenerate, reborn.
In loving you I fell in love with virtue.
For the first time my trembling knees I bend
In humble reverence before it here.

DOÑA ANNA

Ah, that Don Juan is eloquent I know.
I've heard about it, he's a skilled seducer.
They say you are a godless debauchee.

You are a demon. Say, how many women
Have you seduced and ruined?

DON JUAN

I never loved one
Until today.

DOÑA ANNA

So, I am to believe
Don Juan is in love for the first time
And I am more to him than a fresh victim.

DON JUAN

If I had wanted to deceive you, would I
Have told you who I was, pronounced that name
Which must offend your ears? Where do you see
Cold-blooded strategy in that—or cunning?

DOÑA ANNA

With you there is no telling... But how could you
Come here: here where you might be recognised
And nothing then could save you from your death?

DON JUAN

And what is death? For one sweet hour of love
I'd give my life without a murmur.

DOÑA ANNA

How
Will you escape from here, you reckless hothead?

DON JUAN

(kissing her hands)

And you can take thought for poor Juan's life!
Can that mean, Doña Anna, that you bear me
No hatred in your mild, angelic soul?

DOÑA ANNA

If only I could hate you—as I should!
But it is time for you and me to part.

DON JUAN

When shall we meet again?

DOÑA ANNA

I do not know.
Sometime, no doubt.

DON JUAN

Tomorrow?

DOÑA ANNA

Where then?

DON JUAN

Here.

DOÑA ANNA

Ah, how infirm, how frail my heart, Don Juan.

DON JUAN

A kiss of peace in token of forgiveness.

DOÑA ANNA

Enough, now go.

DON JUAN

Just one, so cold, so peaceful...

DOÑA ANNA

There's no contenting you! Come, there you are.
What is that knocking?.. Oh, Don Juan, hide!

DON JUAN

Farewell, until we meet again, dear heart.

Exit and comes running back.

Ah!

DOÑA ANNA

What is it? Ah!

*Enter the COMMANDER'S STATUE;
DOÑA ANNA faints.*

THE STATUE

You called and I have come.

DON JUAN

Oh God! Oh, Doña Anna!

THE STATUE

Leave her be,
This is the end. Don Juan, you are trembling.

DON JUAN

I? No. I did invite you and you're welcome.

THE STATUE

Give me your hand.

DON JUAN

          Here, take it... Ah, how hard
The grip of his stone fingers! Enough, enough,
Leave me alone, let go, let go my hand...
I die—this is the end—ah, Doña Anna!

     They disappear through the floor.

1830

The Water-Nymph

THE BANK OF THE DNIEPER. A MILL

The MILLER, his DAUGHTER.

MILLER

Eh, you are all the same, you giddy maids,
All foolish, scatterbrained. When fortune sends you
A man of rank, an enviable prize,
It's your plain duty to attach him fast.
And how? By sober, virtuous behaviour,
Now strict, now yielding, blowing hot and cold
Upon his passion. Sometimes—just in passing—
A hint at marriage; last, but most important,
To guard your maidenhead, that priceless treasure,
Which, like the spoken word, once it is given
May not be taken back. Or, if there is
No hope of honest wedlock, marriage bells,
Then, even so, and at the least, you should
Get some advantage for your family,
Some slight advancement from it; why, just think,
The old song says: "He will not love me ever
Or seek to please me!" But dear me no, you have
No thought to use your opportunities!
It's not the time, you say, and lose your heads;
You're happy to fulfil his every wish
For nothing, happy to hang upon the neck
Of your true love all day, but your true love
Is here today and gone tomorrow; you—
Left empty-handed; eh, what fools you are.
Haven't I said to you a hundred times:
Now, daughter, you take care, do not be
A fool, don't miss your chances, girl,

Don't let the Prince slip through your fingers,
>   do not
Despoil yourself for nothing. To what end?
Now you may sit and cry your pretty eyes out
For ever. Tears won't bring him back.

DAUGHTER

>   But what
Should make you think that he no longer loves me?

MILLER

What do you mean? But what? How many times
A week used he to visit our poor mill?
Eh? Every blessed day, and sometimes twice
A day—then he began to come more seldom,
More seldom still—and now it's nine whole days
Since he was here. Well, what say you to that?

DAUGHTER

He's busy: do you think he has no duties?
He's not a miller—may not stand and let
The water work for him. He often says
That his work is the hardest in the world.

MILLER

A likely tale. Why, when do Princes work?
What is their work? To hunt the fox, the hare,
To feast, to roister, to browbeat their neighbours,
And to seduce poor ninnies such as you.
He has to work himself; poor, ill-used fellow!
The water works for me, indeed!.. I know
No peace by night or day; always alert!
Now here, now there some new repair is needed,
Now rot, now leaks. If only you had managed
To ask the Prince for just a little money
To put the mill straight, that would have been
>   something.

DAUGHTER

Ah!

MILLER

What is it?

DAUGHTER

I hear the sound of hoof-beats!
His horse's... It is he!

MILLER

Look you, Daughter,
Remember my advice, do not forget.

DAUGHTER

He, here he is.

Enter PRINCE. The groom leads away his horse.

PRINCE

Good morrow, dearest heart.
Good morrow, Miller.

MILLER

Most gracious Prince,
You're welcome. It has been a long, long time
Since we last had a sight of your bright eyes.
I must be off to find you some refreshment.

Exit.

DAUGHTER

Ah, at long last you have remembered me!
Thought you not shame to torture me so long
With empty, cruel anxiety and waiting?
If you had known what thoughts came to my mind!
With what dread fears I harrassed my poor heart!
Sometimes I'd think your horse had bolted with you
Into some quagmire, over some steep cliff,

Or that a bear had killed you in the forest,
That you were ill, that you no longer loved me—
But glory be to God! You're live and well,
And love me still, just as before, my Prince,
Am I not right?

PRINCE

                    Just as before, my angel.
No, better than before—

SHE

                    But you are sad.
What is the matter, love?

PRINCE

                    Do I seem sad?
You have imagined it. No, no, I'm merry
As always at the sight of you, sweet.

SHE

                                No,
When you are merry, you come running to me
And cry while still far off: "Where is my sweetheart,
What is she doing?" Then you kiss me, then
You ask me questions: "Am I glad to see you?
And did I think you would be here so early?"
But now—you listen to me and say nothing,
You do not hug me, do not kiss my eyes;
For sure, you have some worry. What is it?
Is it, perhaps, that you are angry with me?

PRINCE

Indeed, it is unworthy to pretend.
You have guessed right! My heart is heavy now
With sorrow—sorrow which you cannot charm
Away with fond caress or tenderness,
Cannot assuage and cannot even share—

SHE

But it is hurtful to me not to grieve
One grief with you—tell me your secret, Prince.
If you permit it—I shall weep, if not—
No tear of mine shall fall to vex your heart.

PRINCE

Why should I drag it out? The sooner said
The better. Dearest, you must know that in
This world there is no lasting bliss; nor rank,
Nor beauty, neither strength, nor riches—nothing,
Can shelter us from the blind strokes of Fortune.
And we—is it not true, my little sweetheart?—
We had much happiness together. I,
At least, was happy with you, in your love,
And now, whatever may befall me more,
Wherever I may be, I shall remember
You, my dear love; in losing you I lose
A treasure nothing ever will replace.

SHE

I do not quite understand your words,
But I am frightened. Fate holds some threat for us,
Prepares some doom unguessed at, unforeseen.
Not—separation?

PRINCE

                    You have read the riddle.
Fate wills that we should part.

SHE

                              But who should part us?
Can I not follow you wherever you
May go, on foot if need be? I'll go dressed
As a young boy. I'll serve you well and truly
Upon the road, or in the field, at war—
I have no fear of war—if only I
May see you and be near you. No, I will not

Believe it! Either you put me to some test
Or you are teasing me—some empty joke.

PRINCE

No, no, today I have no mind for jokes,
Nor do I need to put you to the test;
Neither am I to ride away to war
Or to far countries, I remain at home,
And yet must part with you, my love, for ever.

SHE

Wait now, I understand it, everything.
You are to wed?

The PRINCE is silent.

You are to wed!

PRINCE

                                    I must.
Put yourself in my place, poor child. A prince
May not obey his heart as young girls may—
He is not free, but chooses in accordance
With calculations made by others for
The good of others... Time and God will comfort
Your sadness; don't forget me; take this headband
In memory of me—I'll put it on.
And I have brought this necklace, too—
Come, take it—this too. I promised it
To your good father. See you give it to him.

He presses a bag of gold into her hand.

Farewell—

SHE

                        One moment. There is something I should...
I have forgotten...

PRINCE

Think.

SHE

For you I would
Do anything ... no, that's not it... Wait, wait—
It cannot be, you could not leave me now
For ever... No. All that's beside the point...
Ah! I have it now: Today your child
Moved for the first time underneath my heart.

PRINCE

Unhappy maid! What can we do? Look after
Yourself if only for his sake; I will not
Abandon either you or your poor child.
In time, may be, I'll even come myself
To visit you. Be comforted. Don't cry.
Come, let me hold you in my arms once more.

(On his way out)

Oof! That is that... A great load off my mind.
I thought there'd be a storm, but things went off
Quite peaceably.

Exit. She remains motionless.

MILLER

(entering)

May I invite you, Prince,
To step inside the millhouse... Where's he gone?
Tell me, where is our Prince? bah, bah, bah! What
A headband! All a-glittering with gems,
It shines like fire! And pearls, too!.. Well,

I must say
That is a royal gift. Ah, benefactor!
And what is that? A bag! Not money, is it?
Why are you standing there not answering,

Without a word to say? Or are you crazed
With joy at such an unexpected windfall,
Or are you struck with lock-jaw?

DAUGHTER

                                        No, I'll not
Believe it, it cannot be. I loved him so.
Or is he a wild beast? Or is his heart
Untame and—shaggy?

MILLER

                        What do you mean, girl?

DAUGHTER

Tell me, my father, what I could have done
To anger him? In one short week is all
My beauty gone? Perhaps he is enchanted
By some vile potion?

MILLER

                        What makes you say so?

DAUGHTER

My father, he is gone.—There, there he gallops!
And I was mad enough to let him go,
I did not clutch his cloak, I did not leap
To grasp his horse's reigns and swing on them!
He might at least have hewn my hands in anger
Hacking them from the wrists, his stallion might
Have trampled me to death beneath his hooves.

MILLER

Have you gone mad?

DAUGHTER

                        But you don't understand...
A prince may not obey his heart as young

Girls may. He is not free to choose ... but he
Is free, it seems, to lure, swear oaths and weep,
To promise: I will take you, sweet, to live
In my fair castle, in a secret solar,
And I shall clothe you in brocades and velvet...
But he is free to teach poor maids to rise
At midnight and come running at his whistle
To sit behind the mill till break of day—
His princely heart is touched by our small woes,
He lends a willing ear to them—and then:
Farewell now, sweetheart, go your ways in peace,
And love who takes your fancy.

MILLER

        Ah, so that's it.

DAUGHTER

But who's to be his bride? For who, I wonder,
Has he exchanged me? Ah, I shall find out,
I'll find the heartless wench, and tell her straight:
You leave the Prince alone, I tell you, two she-wolves
Don't hunt in the same valley.

MILLER

        Silly slut!
If it's the Prince's will to take a bride
Then who's to stop him? Serve you right, I say.
Have I not told you all along...

DAUGHTER

        He could
Take leave of me like a good, kindly man
And give me presents—what d'you think of that!—
And money! Buying himself off, that's it!
He thought to gag me with his gold and silver,
So that no ill repute of him might reach
His youthful princess in her innocence.
Ah yes, I was forgetting; he commanded
To give this bag of coins to you for all

Your kindness to him, that you let your daughter
Trail after him like any drab and set
No strict guard on her virtue... You will be
The gainer by my ruin.

Hands him the bag.

FATHER

(weeping)

My poor, grey hairs!
What have I lived to hear! Shame, shame on you
So bitterly to taunt your aged father.
You are my only child, all that I have,
The only comfort of my feeble age.
I could not help but spoil you, could I now?
The Lord has punished me for lack of firmness
In my parental duty.

DAUGHTER

Ah, I stifle!
A cold snake clings about my neck and squeezes!...
The snake! He has entwined a snake about me,
Not ropes of pearls!..

She tears the pearls from her neck.

MILLER

Think what you're doing!

DAUGHTER

So! and so!
I would tear you to pieces, heartless snake,
Accursed thief of my beloved's heart!

MILLER

You're raving, daughter, raving.

DAUGHTER

(taking off the headband)

> Here's my crown,
A crown of shame! This is the bridal crown
The devil put upon my head when I
Turned me from all that I had once held dear,
Our bridal's over—perish, then, my crown!

She throws the headband into the Dnieper.

Now all is over...

Throws herself into the river.

THE OLD MAN

(falling to the ground)

Oh, horror, horror!

THE PRINCE'S PALACE

*A wedding. The BRIDE and BRIDEGROOM sit at table.
GUESTS. A CHOIR OF YOUNG GIRLS.*

MATCHMAKER

We've made a merry wedding of it, truly.
Your health, then, Prince, and your young bride's,
> our Princess!
God grant you long and happy days together,
And us—good fare and frequent at your table.
Why, lovely maidens, have you fallen silent?
Or have you sung all your sweet songs already?
Or are your white throats dry from too much singing?

CHOIR

Matchmaker, matchmaker
Stupid old matchmaker!

Went to fetch the bride
Missed the way inside,
Out behind the hut
Emptied out a butt
Of beer upon the cabbage-patch
Then fell into the garbage-ditch,
Bowed down to the gate-posts,
"Gate-posts, gentle gate-posts,
Show me pray the way
To fetch the bride today."
Matchmaker, make a guess!
Matchmaker, where's your purse?
In the purse the money's turning
For to treat fair maidens burning.

MATCHMAKER

You rascals, what a song to choose!
There, there, lay off the matchmaker!

Gives the girls money.

A SINGLE VOICE

Where pebbles lie and yellow sands are sifting,
Very swiftly hastened the river.
In the swift river two small fish were swimming,
Two fishes, two small, little roaches.
And have you heard the news, little sister,
The news of what happened in our river?
How that yesterday a fair maid died by drowning,
How she drowned herself and dying cursed her lover?

MATCHMAKER

My beauties! What a song to sing just now!
It's not a wedding song, it's most unfitting,
Who chose that song? Eh?—Who chose it?

THE GIRLS

Not I—

Not I—it wasn't us...

MATCHMAKER

Who sang it then?

Whispering and confusion among the girls.

PRINCE

I know who.

*He leaves the table and quietly issues
instruction to the groom.*

Find the miller's daughter, get her
Away from here—and quickly. Then find out
Who dared admit her.

The groom walks up to the girls.

PRINCE

(sitting down, to himself)

She may well have come
Prepared to kick up such a shindy
I shall not know where to put myself for shame.

GROOM

I could not find her, Prince, amongst the others.

PRINCE

Go. Look again. I know she's there. Her voice
It was that sung that song.

A GUEST

What splendid mead!
It goest straight to the head—and to the legs—
A pity that it's bitter: sweaten it for us.

The bride and bridegroom kiss. A faint cry rings out.

PRINCE

It's she! That was her jealous cry.

(To the groom)

Well,
Found her?

GROOM

I cannot find her anywhere.

PRINCE

You fool.

BEST MAN

(rising)

Is it not time the bride and groom retired
While at the door we shower them with hops?

All rise.

MATCHMAKER

High time, indeed, come, serve the cockerel.

*The bride and bridegroom are served with roast cockerel,
then showered with hops and conducted to their bedroom.*

MATCHMAKER

Sweet Princess, do not cry, don't be afraid,
Do as he says.

*The bride and bridegroom retire to their bedroom, the
guests all take their leave, except for the matchmaker
and the best man.*

BEST MAN

Where is my cup? All night
I have to ride around beneath their windows,
A drop of wine to fortify myself'd
Not come amiss.

MATCHMAKER

(pouring him a cup)

Here, drink this.

BEST MAN

Oof! I thank you.
It all went off quite well, I think, don't you?
The wedding feast was fine—

MATCHMAKER

Yes, God be praised,
All went off well, but one thing was not well.

BEST MAN

Why, what?

MATCHMAKER

It was an evil omen that
They sang that weird song, most unfit for bridals.

BEST MAN

Those wretched girls—they simply can't be trusted
Not to get up to tricks. Who ever heard
Of such a thing! To trouble royal weddings—
On purpose, too... But I must to my horse,
Good night, good gossip.

Exit.

MATCHMAKER

My heart's not easy in me!
This marriage was not made in a good hour.

SOLAR

The PRINCESS and her NURSE.

PRINCESS

Hark—I hear trumpets! No, not yet returned.
Ah, nanny dear, when he was courting me
He never left my side, day after day,
It seemed he could not sate his eyes on me.
He married me, and everything was changed.
Now he wakes me up at crack of dawn
And, as I wake, he's ordering his horse;
Then he rides off, the Lord knows where
                                              till nightfall.
When he comes home he scarcely has a word
Of tenderness for me. He scarce bestows
An absent pat upon my fair, white face.

NURSE

My Little Princess, man is like a rooster:
Cock-a-doo-doo! Flip-flap and off he flies.
A woman, like the modest broody hen,
Must keep her nest and hatch her clutch of chicks.
While he is out to win you he will sit,
Take neither food nor drink, but sit and stare.
Yet once he's married—he's so much to do:
The neighbours must be visited,
He must ride out a-hawking with his falcons,
And then—the Devil's in him—he is off to war.
He's here and there—and everywhere, save home.

PRINCESS

What do you think? Has he perhaps some secret,
Some hidden paramour?—

NURSE

A sin to say so, love:
Where would he find a fair exchange for you?
You have it all: you're wise and beautiful
And gentle in your ways. Why, only think:
Where could he find the match of such as you,
Princess?

PRINCESS

If God would hear my prayers, send
Me children. Then I would have the means
To conquer his affection all anew—
Ah, see, the courtyard's full of huntsmen. He
Is home at last. Why can't I see him, though?

Enter a HUNTSMAN.

Where is the Prince?

HUNTSMAN

He ordered us to leave him
And ride for home.

PRINCESS

But where is he?

HUNTSMAN

Alone
He lingered in the woods that fringe the Dnieper.

PRINCESS

And you dared leave the Prince alone, without
Attendance; what assiduous servants!
Go back at once, this instant, at the gallop,
Tell him that it was I who sent you to him.

Exit the Huntsman.

Ah, gracious heaven! In the woods at night
The haunt of desperate men, wild animals,
And evil spirits—danger everywhere.
Quick, light the candle, here before the icon.

NURSE

At once, my love, at once...

THE DNIEPER. NIGHT

WATER-NYMPHS

A merry procession
From deep in the stream
The moon draws us upward
To bask in her beam.
River floor and water leaving,
Merrily at dead of night,
Glassy surface head-first cleaving
We arise to seek the light.
Hear our voices calling, teasing,
Vibrant through the upper air;
Shaken dry on free winds wreathing,
See our green and dripping hair.

A NYMPH

Sisters, listen, hearken, hush!
In the dark wood something stirs...

ANOTHER

See, between the moon and us
Someone walks upon the earth.

They hide.

PRINCE

How well I know these melancholy places!
I recognise each landmark—there's the mill!

It's fall'n into disuse, a heap of ruins;
The merry sound of turning wheels is silent;
The millstone grinds no more—the old man's dead,
It seems. He did not mourn his hapless daughter
Long. A path wound there... It's overgrown.
For many years no one has come this way.
There was a garden here with a high fence.
Could it have grown into this riot of thicket?
Ah, here's the fatal oak, here's where she stood,
And held me in her arms, all drooping, silent—
Was it all so indeed?..

He goes up to the tree, a shower of leaves falls on him.

What does that mean?
The leaves turned pale before my eyes, curled
round on
Themselves and rustling fell like ashes all
About me. Now the tree stands black and bare
Most like a thing accursed.

An OLD MAN enters, ragged, half-naked.

OLD MAN

Good-day to you,
My son-in-law.

PRINCE

And who are you?

OLD MAN

A raven,
I live here.

PRINCE

Could it be? The miller!

OLD MAN

Not what
I'd call a miller! I have sold my mill

To poltergeists behind the stove, and giv'n the
                                                money
To water-nymphs for keeping, to my daughter,
The wisest of 'em. Now it's buried deep
Down in the Dnieper sand. A one-eyed fish
Keeps guard on it.

PRINCE

              He's mad, unhappy man,
His thoughts are scattered like a storm-spent
                                                cloud.

OLD MAN

You're late. You should have come to us last
                                                night—
We had a feast and waited long for you.

PRINCE

Who waited for me?

OLD MAN

              Who? My lass, who else?
You know I look at all that through my fingers,
You may do as you like: and she may sit
All night with you, till cockcrow, if you wish,
And mum's the word for me.

PRINCE

              Unhappy miller!

OLD MAN

I am no miller, man. I've told you who I am.
A raven, not a miller. Very strange
It was! When she (remember?) flung herself
Into the river, I ran after her
And meant to leap from the same rock, but then
I suddenly felt two strong wings had grown

From 'neath my armpits, and they bore me up
Suspended in the air. And from that day
To this I have been flying about and, now
And then, I peck at carrion—a dead cow, say—
Or perch on graves and caw.

PRINCE

The pity of it!
Who cares for you, old man?

OLD MAN

Now that's a thought!
I need to be taken care of. Getting old
I am and always up to tricks. But I
Must thank my stars I have the water-babe,
She looks to me.

PRINCE

The who?

OLD MAN

My grandchild.

PRINCE

No.
I can't make head or tail of what he says:
Old man, here in the wood you'll die of hunger
Or some beast will devour you. Would you not
Come home with me to live?

OLD MAN

With you? No! Thank you!
You'll lure me in and then, as like as not,
You'll strangle me with pearls. Here I'm alive
And fed and free. I will not go with you.

Exit.

PRINCE

And this is all my doing. Terrible.
To lose one's wits. To die were easier.
We look upon a corpse with due respect,
We pray for him. And death makes all men equal.
A man who's lost his reason is a man
No more, and speech a worthless gift to him,
For he controls not words; a brother he to beasts
And to his fellowmen—a laughing stock;
All folk are free to mock him, no one may judge him,
Not even God! Poor man! The sight of him
Has woke the torments of remorse in me!

HUNTSMAN

Here, here he is. I thought we'd never find him!

PRINCE

Why are you here?

HUNTSMAN

                    The Princess sent us, Sire.
She was afraid for you.

PRINCE

                    Unsufferable
Solicitude. Or am I a small child
Who may not walk a step without a nanny?

Exit. The WATER-NYMPHS rise up from the river.

WATER-NYMPHS

Sisters, shall we overtake them
Lapping round them as they ride,
Scare their horses, spray and shake them,
Whistling, laughing at their side?
No, too late. The forest darkens
And the deep grows colder yet.

To first cockcrow we must hearken,
Look and see, the moon has set.

ONE

Let us tarry here, sweet sister.

ANOTHER

Nay—for we must go, must go,
Summoned by the stern Tsaritsa
Who awaits us down below.

Vanish underwater.

AT THE BOTTOM OF THE DNIEPER

Water-Nymphs' Palace.
The WATER-NYMPHS sit spinning
around the TSARITSA.

TSARITSA

The sun has set, so leave your spinning, sisters.
The moon beams like a pillar through the deep.
Enough, swim up to sport beneath the sky,
But see that you molest no living soul:
Tonight you may not tickle passers-by,
Nor snag the fisherman's wide-spreading net
With grass or weed, nor lure the little child
With tales of fishes down beneath the water...

Enter the WATER-BABE.

Where have you been?

DAUGHTER

                          I've been out on the land
To visit grandfather. He begs me always
To gather up the money that he threw
Into the water to us long ago
And give it back to him. I looked and looked;

Though what this money is I do not know,
But anyway I brought him from the depths,
A handful of bright shells, all different colours,
And he was very pleased.

TSARITSA

The crazy miser!
Now listen, daughter, and attend—this once
I put my trust in you. Tonight a man will come
Down to the river's bank. You will watch out
For him and go to meet him. He is kin
To us—your father, child.

DAUGHTER

The same one who
Abandoned you to wed a mortal woman?

TSARITSA

The same; greet him with tenderness, and tell
Him all you know from me about your birth,
And tell him too what has become of me.
If he should ask you whether I've forgot him
Or not, you may say I remember him
And love him, and invited him to my home.
Now—have you understood me, daughter?

WATER-BABE

I understand.

TSARITSA

Then go.

Alone.

Since that fell hour
When, crazed with grief, I leapt into the water,
A desperate, rejected, simple girl,
And woke again beneath the Dnieper-river,

A waterspirit, cold of heart and potent,
Full seven long years have passed...
And every day I scheme and plan for vengeance.
At last, today, it seems, my hour is come.

THE BANK

PRINCE

Unwillingly to these sad banks I come
Drawn by some unknown power—I know not why...
For me each stick and stone speaks of the past.
Retells the sad but well-beloved tale
Of my young days, my fair and carefree youth.
Here, once upon a time, love waited for me—
Freehearted, ardent love—ah, what a madman
I was to let such joy slip through my fingers,
Renounce such happiness—for I was happy...
How sorrowful, how sorrowful these thoughts.
That meeting yesterday has brought them back.
The poor, mad father! He is terrible.
Perhaps it may be that today I'll meet him
Again and he'll consent to leave the forest
And come to live with us...

The WATER-BABE emerges on the river-bank.

What's this I see!
Say, pretty child, whence came you?

1832

TALES IN VERSE

The Tale of the Fisherman and the Golden Fish

An old man lived with his good-wife
By the shore of the deep blue ocean
In a hovel of clay and wattle;
They had lived there for three years and thirty.
The old man netted fishes,
The good-wife sat at her spinning.
Once he cast his net on the waters;
The net came up—full of sea-slime.
Again he cast the net on the waters;
The net came back—full of sea-weed.
A third time the net sank in the waters
And came up with one fish in it.
No common fish, but a golden.
The golden fish begged for mercy
And spoke with the voice of a human:
"Old man, throw me back in the ocean,
I will pay you a splendid ransom:
I will grant you whatever you wish for."
The old man was amazed and awestruck:
He had fished here for three years and thirty
But never once heard a fish talking.
Freeing the fish from the meshes
He gave him fair words and gentle:
"Golden fish, go your ways in peace now
There is no need to pay me a ransom;
Go back to your deep blue seas
And swim there and splash as you please."

The old man returned to his good-wife
And told her of this great wonder:
"Today I netted a strange fish
No common fish, but a golden;
The golden fish spoke our language,
Begged to go home to the ocean,
Promised a splendid ransom:
To grant me whatever I wished for.
I durstn't exact the ransom;
Threw him back in the sea for nothing."
The wife fell to scolding her husband:
"Simpleton, silly old fat-head!
Too soft to get boons of fishes!
A new wash-trough at least you might ask for,
Ours is split right down the middle!"

He went back to the deep blue ocean.
He saw that the ocean was ruffled.
Then he raised his voice and shouted,
And the golden fish came swimming;
"What is it, old man, come tell me!"
With a low bow, the old man made answer:
"Be gracious, Lord of Fishes,
My good-wife is angry with me,
And gives me no peace with her nagging;
She says that we need a new wash-trough;
Ours is split right down the middle."
The golden fish made answer:
"Never mind, old man, go in peace now,
You will find a new wash-trough all ready."
The old man returned to his good-wife,
To find the new wash-trough all ready.
But she scolded him now worse than ever:
"Simpleton! Silly old fat-head!
So you begged a great boon—a new wash-trough!
But what profit is there in a wash-trough?
Back, you simpleton, you, to the great fish,
Make your bow to him: ask for an *izba**."

He went back to the deep blue ocean
(The ocean was dark now and troubled).

Izba—Russian peasant's log cabin.

Then he raised his voice and shouted,
And the golden fish came swimming:
"What is it, old man, come, tell me!"
With a low bow, the old man made answer:
"Be gracious, Lord of Fishes!
My good-wife is even more angry.
And gives me no peace with her nagging:
The old ne'er content wants an *izba*."
The golden fish made answer:
"Never mind, old man, go in peace now,
You shall have your wish: a new *izba*."
The old man returned to his hovel;
Not a trace remained of the hovel;
In its place—a brand-new *izba*
With whitewashed, brickwork chimney,
Oaken doors, a carved attic window.
On the garden seat sat his good-wife
Quite beside herself this time with anger:
"What a fool you are, simpleton, fat-head!
So you begged a great boon, a low *izba*!
Go back, make your bow to the great fish:
I will not be a plain peasant woman,
Let him make me a high-born lady."

The old man went down to the ocean
(The ocean was rough now and choppy).
Then he raised his voice and shouted,
And the golden fish came swimming:
"What is it, old man, come, tell me!"
With a low bow, the old man made answer:
"Be gracious, Lord of Fishes!
My good-wife's more wilful than ever
And gives me no peace with her nagging;
And now she has taken a notion
That she'll not be a plain peasant woman
But will be a high-born lady."
The golden fish made answer:
"Never mind, old man, go in peace now."

The old man returned to his good-wife.
And what does he see? A fine mansion.
On the porch his good-wife is standing,
Her rich jacket trimmed with sable,

A high, brocaded head-dress,
Pearls on her neck hanging heavy,
Golden rings on her fingers
And boots of soft, red leather.
Before her, servants are bowing;
She pulls their hair and strikes them.
The old man hailed his good-wife:
"How now, Mistress-Madam-M'lady,
Surely your heart is content now?"
His good-wife greeted him harshly,
And sent him to serve in the stables.

A week went by, then another,
And the good-wife, more self-willed than ever,
Sent the old man back to the ocean.
"Go back, make your bow to the great fish:
Say I'll not be a high-born lady.
Let him make me a mighty Empress."
The old man took fright, and argued:
"What, woman! You must be moon-struck!
You talk and you walk like a fishwife,
You will set your whole Empire laughing."
The good-wife grew still more angry,
Boxed her husband's ears and shouted:
"How dare you argue, you peasant,
With me, with a high-born lady?
Get you gone to the sea, I tell you,
Unless you want to be dragged there."

The old man went back to the ocean
(Black and threatening now, the blue ocean).
Then he raised his voice and shouted,
And the golden fish came swimming:
"What is it, old man, come, tell me!"
With a low bow the old man made answer:
"Be gracious, Lord of Fishes!
Again my good-wife's on the rampage;
This time, she's taken a notion
That she'll not be a high-born lady
But will be a mighty Empress."
And the golden fish made answer:
"Never mind, old man, go in peace now!
You will find your good-wife an Empress!"

The old man returned to his good-wife.
And what do you think? A palace
Now houses the shrewish old woman.
She sits in state at her table.
Great nobles and lords wait upon her,
Serve her wine in a golden goblet
While she nibbles at crested sweet-meats;
Stern sentries mount guard about her
Each with an axe at the ready.
The old man took one look—his knees failed him!
He bowed to the ground before her
But spoke out: "All hail, dread Empress!
Tell me, is your heart content now?"
Not a glance did his good-wife spare him
But ordered her men to remove him.
Then the lords and great nobles came running,
By the scruff of the neck they took him,
And the sentries who stood in the doorways
Saw him off with their axes,
And the people shamed him with laughter.
"Serve you right, witless old grey-beard!
Let that be a lesson to you
To remember your place in future!"

So a week went by, then another.
The old woman grew more and more grasping.
She sent courtiers to fetch the old man.
They found him, brought him before her.
Then the good-wife said to her husband:
"Go back, make your bow to the great fish.
I'll no more be a mighty Empress
But will rule over Sea and Ocean.
In the Deep I will make my stronghold
And the golden fish shall serve me
And swim back and forth on my errands."
The old man dared not contradict her,
Was afraid to stand up against her.
Again he went down to the ocean
And saw—a black storm had arisen:
Angry waves reared up to meet him,
All a-quake, all a-swirl, all a-roaring.
But he raised his voice and shouted,
And the golden fish came swimming:

"What is it, old man, come, tell me!"
With a low bow the old man made answer:
"Be gracious, Lord of Fishes!
What can I do with the woman?
The old fool will no longer be Empress,
She will rule over Sea and Ocean;
In the Deep she will make her stronghold
And have you yourself to serve her
And swim back and forth on her errands."
The golden fish said nothing;
With a flick of its tail in the water
It swam away, back to the deep sea.
The old man by the shore stood waiting
For a long time, but got no answer.
At last, he returned to his good-wife
And lo: there she sat on the threshold
Of their old hut of clay and wattle
And before her—the broken wash-trough.

1833

The Tale of the Golden Cockerel

In a thrice-nine realm that lay
O'er the seas and far away
Lived and reigned the great Dadon.
In his youth he had been known
For his ruthless ways and fierce,
But in later, riper years,
Wearying of war and strife,
Showed a fondness for a life
Of repose and calm...
                              Alas!
By his neighbours now he was
Teased and harassed: oft did they
Overrun his lands. At bay
For to hold them old Dadon
Had to keep large armies on
All his borders, near and far.
But the captains of the Tsar
Proved, to his alarm, too slow
For the nimble-footed foe:
Thought in all good faith to be
Southward bound, he suddenly
Was encountered in the east,
Or, when there expected least,
Would at sea be sighted...
                              Poor
Tsar Dadon could ill endure
Such reverse. He wept in rage,
Lost his sleep, and for a sage,
An astrologer and seer,
Sent at last in hope and fear.

With a bow the mage is shown
Into the presence of Dadon,
And from out his sack—behold!—
Brings he forth a Cock of gold,
Saying, "Heed my counsel, Sire,
Place the Cock atop a spire,
And on guard he'll faithful stand
Of your great and mighty land.
While there's peace, O Tsar, he will
On his perch keep very still.
But if there be threat of war,
Or a hint of evil, or
Should on you a sudden raid
By the enemy be made,
Then the Cock his wings will spread,
Lift his golden, crested head
And with loud and piercing crow
Give you warning where the foe
Thinks to strike."
                                    "I do declare,"
Said the Tsar, well pleased, "that ne'er
Heard I better words or braver.
Honest wizard, of my favour
Rest assured. Whate'er you will,
That shall I at once fulfil."

Perched atop a turret steep,
Sleepless watch the Cock did keep
O'er the land, but, so we learn,
If alarmed, at once would turn
Toward the side whence danger came
And address Dadon by name
Cruing, "Cock-a-doodle-doo!
I have this to say to you:
Lie abed, o Tsar, and reign."
And—O joy!—Dadon's domain
Was attacked and stormed no more
And for once could rest from war.

Thus a year or two went by
Till a sudden hue and cry
In the early hours of dawn
Roused the sleeping Tsar Dadon.

"Wake, O Tsar our father, pray!"
Called his *voyevoda**. "Eh?"
Yawned Dadon and opened an eye.
"What's this awful clamour?" "Why,
'Tis the Cock. He's crowing, Sire,
Loud as loud atop the spire;
All are up and in a fright..."
To the window for a sight
Of the Cock Dadon now hurried.
Eastward was the badly flurried
Sentry facing as he crowed.
Cried Dadon, for this did bode
Nothing good: "Ho, men, to horse!"
And he sent a mighty force,
With his first-born at its head,
War to wage.
        As off they sped,
On his perch the Cockerel
Ceased to crow and silent fell.

Eight full days went by but no
Tidings came from friend or foe.
Had a battle taken place
Or had they one still to face?..
As the fear and panic grew,
Loud the Cock shrilled out anew.
Tsar Dadon, by wisdom led,
Sent his younger son at head
Of a second host in search
Of the first.
        Upon his perch,
Hushed and still, for eight whole days
Sat the Cock. With anxious gaze
Tsar and townsfolk watched him, till
Once again that rousing shrill
Rang above the palace. Then
Tsar Dadon a host of men
Did himself without delay
Call to arms and straightaway
Lead them eastward...
        On they went,

Voyevoda—commander of an army.

On their wearing mission bent,
But no camp, no battle-ground,
Not a barrow or a mound
Met upon the way. At last,
When a week and day had passed,
'Fore a gorge surrounded by
Hills whose summits scraped the sky
And where stood a silken tent
They arrived, worn out and spent.
All around in disarray
Torn and broken bodies lay.
Tsar Dadon in sudden dread
Nearer drew... Before him, dead,
By each other's swords pierced through,
Lay his sons, his falcons two,
With their steeds, of movement shy,
Wandering in the field nearby,
O'er the crushed and bloody grass...
"O, that this should come to pass!"
Cried Dadon, and beat his breast.
"That my sons, my own two blest
Falcons should be trapped and die
In this wise... Indeed, 'tis my
Death has come, and all is lost!"
Joining in, the Tsar's brave host
Wailed with him... A heavy sigh
From the hills came in reply.
Of a sudden out the tent,
To Dadon's great wonderment,
Stepped a maid, Tsarina of
Shamakhan, the skies above
With her dazzling beauty shaming.
Like a night-bird by the flaming
Orb of day, so was he dazed
And, enthralled, upon her gazed,
Sons and host forgot... The maid
Smiled most sweetly, and with staid
Bow she led him by the hand
To her tent and there in grand,
Nay, e'en more,—in sumptuous style
Fêted him. So did they while
Half the merry night away,
After which, at break of day,

On a bed of gold brocade
For to rest him he was laid...
Thus, bewitched, entranced, content,
With the maid a week he spent.

But at last the week was done
And for home the good Dadon
Set him out with host and maid,
While ahead, by none delayed,
Old Dame Rumour swiftly flew,
Spreading fact and fable, too.

At Dadon's own gate a crowd
Met the Tsar and ran with loud
Cheers behind the royal pair,
And the two with gracious air
Smiled and waved...
                Amid the throng
Which was many hundreds strong
Now did Tsar Dadon espy
In a turban with a high
Snow-white top his friend the seer
Whom at once he beckoned near.
To the bearded ancient thus
Spake Dadon: "Pray, answer us:
Is there aught you wish for, sage?"
Said the man: "You did engage
To repay your debt to me,
Promising most faithfully
For to do what I desire.
Hear my wish and grant it, Sire:
The Tsarina for my own
I would have." At this Dadon
Stood aghast. Cried he: "Egad!
Good my man, you must be mad,
This may lead to your undoing...
Surely 'tis the devil's doing
And naught else... I won't deny,
Give my word I did, but why
Ask for something you don't need?
Put a limit on your greed
And go not, I beg, too far—
You forget that I am Tsar!

Be a *boyar**, if you will,
With my gold your coffers fill,
Take my horse for you to ride,
Half my tsardom take beside."
"Nay," the eunuch answered him,
"Call it fancy, call it whim,
But I'll have the young Tsarina."
"What?!" Dadon exclaimed. "You sinner!"
And in towering rage he spat
On the ground. "Now just for that
You'll get nothing, do you hear?
Guards, remove him!" But the seer
Trying vainly to protest,
And with some 'tis surely best
To refrain from arguing,
Tsar Dadon his staff did bring
Down upon the ancient's head,
Whereupon the mage dropped dead.
The whole town was thunderstruck...
But the maid showed wondrous pluck.
"Ha-ha-ha!" laughed she. "Tee-hee!"
And the Tsar, though pained was he,
Beamed at her...
                        As through the gate
They moved slowly on in state,
To the marvel of the town,
From his spire the Cock came down,
On the Tsar's bald pate alighted,
Gave a peck, and, nothing frighted,
Flew away...
                        With broken moan
From his chariot Dadon
Rolled and breathed his last forthwith,
While the maid he'd come there with
Vanished and no more was seen,
Just as if she'd never been...

To you all, my lads, and each
Let this tale a lesson teach.

1834

Boyar—calling conferred on a man, making him a member of an aristo-
cratic order.

A miniature made of Pushkin in his infancy

Moscow in the year of Pushkin's birth.
A view of Chudov Palace in the Kremlin.
An engraving. 1799

Sergei Pushkin (1770–1848), the poet's father.
Crayons. 1810s

Nadezhda Pushkina, *née* Hannibal (1775–1836),
the poet's mother.
A miniature. Early nineteenth century

Pushkin at the age of thirteen.
An engraving enclosed with the first edition of the poem
"The Captive in the Caucasus". 1822

Vassily Pushkin (1767–1830). A poet and Alexander's uncle on the father's side. He brought his nephew from Moscow to St. Petersburg in 1811 for enrollment in the Lyceum. A lithograph. 1810s

The Yekaterininsky Palace in Tsarskoye Selo near St. Petersburg. The Lyceum where Pushkin received his education was housed in the left wing of the Palace. A lithograph. 1822

Yekaterina Bakunina (1795–1869). The sister of Pushkin's schoolmate, and his first love to whom he dedicated more than 30 poems of the Lyceum period. A drawing. 1810s

Anton Delwig (1798–1831). Pushkin's
schoolmate. A poet. One of Pushkin's
closest and best-loved friends.
A lithograph. 1831

Ivan Pushchin (1799–1859). Pushkin's closest friend from the Lyceum days. In a poem
dedicated to him Pushkin addressed him as
"My first, my dearest friend". For participation in the Decembrist uprising Pushchin
was sentenced to hard labour in Siberia.
From a lithograph of the 1820s

Gavriil Derzhavin (1743–1816). A famous Russian
poet who at the close of his days saluted young
Pushkin as the rising star of Russian poetry.
A portrait by Borovikovsky. 1811

Pushkin reciting his verses at a public examination
in the Lyceum (in presence of Derzhavin) in 1815.
A painting by Repin. 1911

Konstantin Batyushkov (1787–1855). A poet,
much admired by young Pushkin.
An engraving. 1821

Pyotr Chaadayev (1794–1856). A writer and philosopher who greatly influenced the shaping of Pushkin's world outlook. A portrait by Molinari. 1810s

St. Petersburg. Nevsky Prospekt with a view
of the Admiralty. A lithograph. 1820s

Vassily Zhukovsky (1783–1852). A poet. Pushkin's elder
contemporary and friend, who, in 1820, presented him with
the portrait which had an inscription: "To the victorious
pupil from the vanquished teacher". A lithograph. 1820

Gurzuf, the Crimea. In the right bottom corner is the house
where Pushkin lived in 1820. A lithograph. 1822

The Fountain of Tears in the Bakhchisarai Palace,
described in Pushkin's famous poem.
A lithograph. 1840s

Maria Volkonskaya (1805–1863) with her son.
The daughter of General Rayevsky and the wife
of Prince Sergei Volkonsky, who took part in the
Decembrist uprising. In 1826 she renounced all
nobiliary rights and privileges and followed her
husband into Siberian exile. Pushkin was in love
with young Maria and later greatly admired
the civic heroism of this woman. A water-colour
by Sokolov. 1826

Yelizaveta Vorontsova (1792–1880). The wife
of Count Vorontsov. In the 1820s Pushkin
addressed numerous love lyrics to her.
An engraving. 1829

Vera Vyazemskaya (1790–1886).
The wife of Prince Vyazemsky,
and Pushkin's great friend.
A miniature. 1809

The seaport of Odessa. Pushkin lived
in this town in 1823–1824. A picture
by Aivazovsky. 1840s

Mikhailovskoye, the estate of Pushkin's mother. He spent more than two years in exile here. A lithograph. 1837

Arina Rodionovna (1758–1828), Pushkin's nurse. The Hannibals, whose serf she was, gave her her freedom in 1799. This illiterate but naturally gifted Russian woman knew a great many folk songs, legends, and fairy-tales, and Pushkin used some of them in his work. In the poem "To My Nanny" Pushkin addrssed her in these words: "Dear doting sweetheart of my childhood, companion of my austere fate..." A bas-relief. 1840s

Bridge in the Mikhailovskoye park

Pushkin at Mikhailovskoye.
A painting by Ulyanov

Ivan Pushchin visiting the poet in Mikhailovskoye in 1826.
A picture by Ghé. 1875

Anna Kern (1800–1879). A society beauty with whom
Pushkin was infatuated and to whom he addressed
one of his most stirring love poems. Pushkin's drawing.
1829

Osipov's house in Trigorskoye, a village neighbouring on Mikhailovskoye.
Pushkin often visited his friends the Osipovs here. A lithograph. 1899

A. Pushkin. 1831. The unknown artist

Pushkin with his wife at a ball.
A painting by Ulyanov

Wilhelm Küchelbecker (1797–1846). Pushkin's friend from the Lyceum days, a poet. For participation in the Decembrist uprising he was kept prisoner for ten years and then exiled to Siberia where he went blind and died. Pushkin's first poem to appear in print, "To My Poet Friend" (1814), was addressed to Küchelbecker. An engraving of the late nineteenth century

Kondraty Ryleyev (1795–1826), a poet. As the leader of the Decembrist uprising, he was executed by hanging. A miniature. 1820s

The Decembrist uprising on 14th December 1825, in Senate Square,
St. Petersburg. Water-colours. 1825

A sheet of Pushkin's manuscript with drawings of the execution
of the Decembrists and the following words:
"I, too, might have..." 1826

Zinaida Volkonskaya (1792–1862). A poetess, composer and
singer. In 1820s Pushkin frequented her famous salon in Moscow.
An engraving. 1814

Moscow, Tverskoi Boulevard. A lithograph. 1830s

Moscow, Bolshaya Nikitskaya Street. A lithograph. 1830s

Yevgeny Baratynsky (1800–1844). An elegiac poet who
was highly valued by Pushkin.
A lithograph. 1828

Alexandra Muravyova (1804–1832). The wife of the Decembrist
Nikita Muravyov, who followed her husband to exile in Siberia.
It was with her that Pushkin sent the Decembrists his famous
poem "Deep in Siberia's mines, let naught..." A lithograph. 1826

Pushkin's manuscript of the poem *The Gypsies* with his drawings.
1823

The flood in St. Petersburg in 1824 described by Pushkin
in his poem *The Bronze Horseman*.
An engraving. 1824

St. Petersburg. Senate Square, with a view of the monument
to Peter the Great. A coloured engraving. 1806

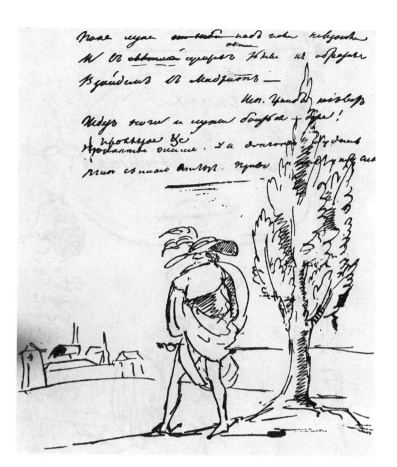

The manuscript of Pushkin's drama *The Stone Guest*
witn his drawings. 1830

The title page of Pushkin's manuscript
of *The Tale of the Golden Cockerel* with his drawings. 1834

NOTES

To Chaadayev (p. 9)

This poem, addressed to one of Pushkin's closest friends P. Y. Chaadayev (1794-1856), a progressive thinker and enlightener, enjoyed exceptional popularity.

"Light wanes, in sudden haste retreating..." (p. 10)

As seen from Pushkin's letter to his brother, he wrote this elegy during his voyage from Feodosia to Gurzuf: "We sailed along the sunlit shores of Taurida to Gurzuf... That night, on board ship, I wrote an elegy."

The Captive (p. 13)

In all probability what prompted Pushkin to write this poem was his visit to the Kishinev prison. Set to music, it made a beautiful song.

Farewell to the Sea (p 15.)

Pushkin began writing this in Odessa and finished it when he was leaving for a new stretch of exile in the village of Mikhailovskoye.

a tomb of glory—St. Helena where Napoleon died in exile.

another bold and mighty genius—Lord Byron who died on April 19, 1824 in Greece where he went to aid the Greeks in their battle for national independence.

To*** (p. 19)

Dedicated to Anna Kern whom Pushkin first met in St. Petersburg in 1819. He met her again in the summer of 1825 when he was in exile in Mikhailovskoye and she came to stay with friends in Trigorskoye, a neighbouring estate.

Winter Evening (p. 20)

Dedicated to Pushkin's old nurse Arina Rodionovna about whom the poet wrote in a letter from Mikhailovskoye where he lived in banishment: "In the evenings I listen to the tales told me by my nurse... She is my only friend, and only with her I do not feel dull."

The Prophet (p. 23)

Written in the style of the *Book of Isaiah* who hated kings, exposed their lawlessness and for this was executed. According to Pushkin's contemporaries he had written three more poems in this vein, but they have not been preserved. He wrote the present one upon learning of the hanging of five Decembrists.

"Deep in Siberia's mines, let naught..." (p. 27)

Addressed to the Decembrists sentenced to hard labour in Siberia.

A. Odoyevsky replied to this poem with one of his own which began:

> *The magic sounds of strings prophetic*
> *Have, warm and rousing, reached our ear!*
>
> Translated by Irina Zheleznova.

Arion (p. 28)

This poem, written on July 16, 1827, most certainly has a bearing on the first anniversary of the execution of the five Decembrists (July 13, 1826). In it Pushkin allegorically describes his relations with the members of the Decembrist movement. Arion, according to popular legend, was a poet and musician in ancient Greece, who was saved from perishing in the sea by a dolphin, charmed by his music.

"Sing, lovely one, I beg, no more..." (p. 29)

The composer Mikhail Glinka said that Pushkin had written this poem "to the tune of a Georgian melody which he chanced to hear A. Olenina (one of Glinka's pupils) sing".

Fatal shadow—apparently a reference to M. N. Rayevskaya-Volkonskaya.

Antiar (p. 30)

Antiar, the upas tree of Java whose juice was used as an arrow poison.

When the poem was reprinted Pushkin substituted the word *prince* for *tsar*, obviously being compelled to make the change because the original publication had roused such sharp displeasure in Benkendorf, the chief of the Gendarmerie.

"Upon the hills of Georgia lies the haze of night..." (p. 32)

It is obvious from the first version of the poem, preserved in manuscript, that Pushkin was inspired by his recollections of the first time he went to the Caucasus in the summer of 1820 together with the family of General Rayevsky, and of his passion for M. N. Rayevskaya-Volkonskaya.

"I loved you, and that love..." (p. 35)

It is not known to whom this poem was addressed.

The Caucasus (p. 38)

The poem was prompted by Pushkin's travel impressions during his journey to Erzerum.

"When in my arms your slender form..." (p. 39)

Addressed to Natalia Goncharova, the poet's future wife.

"What means my name to you?.." (p. 40)

Pushkin wrote this in the album of Karolina Sobańska, a celebrated beauty.

" 'Tis time, my friend, 'tis time!.." (p. 49)

In this poem, addressed to his wife, Pushkin expresses his ardent desire to retire, quit St. Petersburg, and get away from the court and from society, to settle in the country, wholly devoting himself to writing.

"A monument I've raised not built with hands..." (p. 52)

The epigraph is taken from Horatio's ode "To Melpomene". By *Alexander's Column* Pushkin means the Triumphal Column erected in Palace Square in St. Petersburg as a monument to Russia's victory in the war of 1812 during the reign of Alexander I. In Pushkin's manuscript the fourth verse had a more political ring:

> *And long the people yet will reverence me*
> *Because new harmonies in song I found,*
> *And, like Radishchev, sang of liberty,*
> *And let my lyre to mercy's praise resound.*

Translated by Avril Pyman.

The Gypsies (p. 55)

Pushkin began writing this poem in January 1824, and before his banishment to Mikhailovskoye from Odessa he had 145 verses written in the rough. He resumed work on the poem after he had been in Mikhailovskoye for about two months, and finished it very quickly.

Handwritten copies of this poem, infused with a longing for freedom and a hatred for the social and political system of the time, "as dreary as the song of slaves", were widely circulated and became extremely popular among the Decembrists. In a letter dated March 25, 1825, Ryleyev wrote to Pushkin: "Everyone is raving about your *Gypsies*." Apparently, the situation after the defeat of the Decembrist uprising was such that Pushkin was obliged to put off the publication of *The Gypsies*, and the poem only appeared in print in book form in 1827. The name of the author was not mentioned, and it simply said: "Written in 1824".

A legend that has never vanished—the reference here is to Ovid, the exiled Roman poet.

The Bronze Horseman (p. 75)

Written in October 1833 in Boldino, this was a summing up of the poet's meditations on the historical destinies of Russia. And it was the last long poem that Pushkin was to write.

Peter the Great is presented as a dialectically complex character—he is shown as a great reformer, a tsar who consolidated Russia's statehood, yet he is also "the grim and haughty idol" of autocracy who ruthlessly tramples on everything that stands in his way. This instantly put Tsar Nicholas I who was Pushkin's "royal censor" on his guard. There is this entry in Pushkin's diary made on December 14, 1833, the 8th anniversary of the Decembrist uprising, which says: "My *Bronze Horseman* has been returned to me with the tsar's remarks. The word *idol* was barred by the royal censorship. The following verse was struck out:

> *Old Moscow fades beside her rival:*
> *A dowager, she is outshone*
> *O'ershadowed by the new arrival,*
> *Who, robed in purple, mounts the throne.*

See p. 76 of this volume.
A question mark was put against many lines, and all this makes a great difference." If all the changes demanded by the tsar were made, the profound historico-political meaning of the poem would be weakened considerably, and so Pushkin decided not to have it published for the time being. During his lifetime only the "Introduction" was published. Three years after this, Pushkin wanted to

try and get the poem printed in his journal *Sovremennik*, and began changing in part the places marked off by the tsar. He changed the word *idol* to *rider*, and slightly altered the main part describing Yevgeny's "mutiny" against Peter the Great which virtually bristled with the tsar's question marks and irritable comments. As for the theme of "mutiny", the poet left it intact. After Pushkin's death, the task of revising the poem was finished for him by Zhukovsky.

The flood described in the poem occurred in St. Petersburg on November 7, 1824, and caused enormous destruction. Pushkin, who was in Mikhailovskoye at the time, took the calamity very much to heart and anxiously tried to find out all the details. In a letter to his brother dated December 4, 1824, he wrote: "The flood is on my mind all the time." He considered the measures under- taken by the government to aid the flood victims utterly inadequate, and added: "If it occurs to you to help one of these unfortunates, use *Onegin's* money (i. e., the money which Pushkin had received for the publication of the first chapter of *Eugene Onegin—Ed.*), and mind there's no blowing of trumpets, either in words or in writing."

The Covetous Knight (p. 91)

The plot for this play was evidently conceived by Pushkin as far back as in 1826 when he was in Mikhailovskoye. Pushkin finished writing it on October 23, 1830, in Boldino. Apparently, fearing that the play would be interpreted as an autobiography (it was an open secret that his father was a miser and that there was no love lost between them), Pushkin presented it as a translation from a non- existent original. William Shenstone (1714-1763), the English poet to whom Pushkin ascribed the original, had never written the drama. Probably this was why Pushkin kept putting off the printing of his play: it was only published in 1836 in the first issue of Pushkin's journal *Sovremennik* signed with the letter *P*. The premiere was to be held at the Alexandrinsky Theatre in St. Petersburg on February 13, 1837 (Pushkin died three days earlier). However, the authorities, fearing a public demonstration of sympathy with the murdered poet and hatred for those guilty of his death, had the premiere cancelled and a vaudeville shown instead that night.

In the manuscript Pushkin called by play *The Miser*, with a sub- title in English *The Covetous Knight*.

Mozart and Salieri (p. 111)

The plot was conceived in 1826 in Mikhailovskoye, and the play was finished on October 26, 1830, in Boldino. Originally Pushkin wanted to call it *Jealousy* and this is borne out by the note he made early in the 1830s.

"During the first performance of *Don Giovanni* when the entire audience, filled with amazed connoisseurs, listened rapturously to Mozart's harmony, someone whistled. Everyone turned toward the sound with indignation, and saw the famous Salieri leaving the hall in a fury, devoured by jealousy. Salieri died eight years or so ago. Some German magazines said that on his deathbed Salieri confessed to the terrible crime of poisoning the great Mozart. A jealous man who was capable of catcalling *Don Giovanni*, was capable of poisoning the maker of this music."

The news that Antonio Salieri (1750-1825) had confessed on his deathbed to poisoning Mozart was printed in many European newspapers in 1825, and prompted Pushkin to write his drama. Salieri's friends considered it their duty to come out in defence of the composer's honour and clear his name, and declared that he made his admission in a moment of mental derangement. Poet P. A. Katenin censured Pushkin for basing his play on a false charge. Still, some present-day researchers prove that Salieri was, in fact, guilty of the crime.

Mozart and Salieri was Pushkin's only play staged in his lifetime. (It was shown in St. Petersburg on January 27 and February 1, 1832.)

Iphigenia the reference is to one of Glück's operas.

Voi che sapete—from the aria of Cherubino in Mozart's *Le Marriage de Figaro*.

Tarare—opera by Salieri to words by Beaumarchais.

And Buonarotti?—this is a reminder of the unfounded legend that Michelangelo Buonarotti, the great Italian artist, had stabbed his model with a knife in order to give a true-to-life rendering of Christ's death agonies.

The Stone Guest (p. 122)

Pushkin conceived the plot in 1826 in Mikhailovskoye, and finished writing the play on November 4, 1830, in Boldino. On March 1, 1828, he wrote into the album of the Polish pianist Szymanowska three verses from his future drama:

> ...*Of all life's pleasures*
> *Music yields pride of place to love alone,*
> *And even love's—a melody...*

See p. 130 of this volume.

In this play Pushkin gives his own, very original interpretation of the image of Don Juan, presenting him as a poet of passion.

The epigraph was borrowed from the libretto written for Mozart's opera *Don Giovanni* by Da Ponte.

And the night watch calls his longdrawn: "sereno!"—night watchmen in Spain who were called serenos (from the word *sereno* —calm) had to call out the time and the weather at regular intervals.

The Water-Nymph (p. 159)

Pushkin conceived the plot while in exile in Mikhailovskoye in 1826, and actually wrote the play between November 1829 and April 1832. In his manuscript the play has no title, and it was called *The Water-Nymph* by *Sovremennik* where it was first published in 1837.

The Tale of the Fisherman and the Golden Fish (p. 187)

This tale was written in 1833 in Boldino. Pushkin finished it on October 14, 1833.

The Tale of the Golden Cockerel (p. 193)

Pushkin's clean copy is dated "Boldino, September 20, 1834, 10 hours 53 minutes." Foreseeing inevitable trouble with the censors, Pushkin made certain changes in the text before handing the tale in for print. For example, in the lines *and with tsars 'tis surely best to refrain from arguing...* he replaced the word *tsars* with *some*. This last amendment was most significant, for at the time Pushkin's quarrel with the tsar was a most topical theme for him.

Александр Пушкин

ИЗБРАННЫЕ ПРОИЗВЕДЕНИЯ. ПОЭЗИЯ

На английском языке

Подробнее ознакомиться с содержанием
и оформлением наших книг можно по Интернету.
Наш адрес: **www.raduga.express.ru**

Оформление *Е. Кузнецовой*
Художественный редактор *Т. Иващенко*

Подписано в печать 09.10.2000.
Формат 84 × 100/32. Бумага офсетная.
Печать офсетная. Условн. печ. л. 12,09. Уч.-изд. л. 9,82.
Доп. тираж 3000 экз. Заказ № 1928. Изд. № 8880.

Налоговая льгота – общероссийский классификатор
продукции ОК-005-93, том 2;
953000 – книги, брошюры.

Лицензия ЛР № 020846 от 23 декабря 1998 г.
ОАО Издательство «Радуга»
121839, Москва, пер. Сивцев Вражек, 43.

Отпечатано
в ОАО «Можайский полиграфический комбинат»
143200, г. Можайск, ул. Мира, 93.